A Spiritual Walkabout

Memoirs of a journey from religion to spirituality

In Memoriam

Muffy and Robin

A Spiritual Walkabout

Published by Englishcombe Press,
an imprint of Celestial Voices, Inc.
13354 W. Heiden Circle,
Lake Bluff, IL 60044 USA

Cover design: Robert Buzek Designs Inc.

Library of Congress Control Number: 2014922905

ISBN: 978-0-9836016-9-2 (paperback)
See also
ISBN: 9788-0-9912638-2-0 (e-book)

FIRST EDITION

Note:
This book contains matter from a little-circulated ebook, *Disarming Death,* now unavailable.

Millions are quietly leaving churches, temples, and mosques

A Spiritual Walkabout

My journey from religion to spirituality

Peter Watson Jenkins

Englishcombe Press

Advertisement

Training for the Marathon of Life

"I wanted so much to write this book," says Peter Watson Jenkins. "It puts into print concepts that were important to me on my spiritual walkabout. As I became more radical and felt more able to express myself, it finally dawned that it was okay to risk the judgment others might make— who said that I was not a real theologian and should leave writing about Jesus to those who understood him. But I did understand him! He wanted those who took his words seriously to create a grass roots movement that he called The Kingdom."

Entry into the kingdom, Peter explains, requires people to break free from the past and make several major changes in their lifestyle, if needed. Jesus spelled them out. They are all in familiar individual sayings to us, but we do not understand that his teaching was a complete blueprint made for anybody to follow. The personal changes he asked for would be very tough for some people to make, but they were essential if we were to belong to the community of the Kingdom (that Peter has christened The Good Society). We have failed to understand that Jesus had created a virtual handbook to guide us in our living together in society. This may well be the cause of Christians' failure to convince the rest of the world that they really do know how Jesus wanted us all to live.

Training for the Marathon of Life (ISBN: 1597524476) by Peter Watson Jenkins is published in a small paperback by Resource Publications (an Imprint of Wipf and Stock, publishers) 199 West 8th Avenue, Eugene, OR 97401. It is currently available from Amazon and other booksellers.

P.S. Lots of sermon material for clergy. Great for group discussions!

Contents

A Spiritual Walkabout

Walkabouts and Dreamtime

The Australian Aborigine's historic "walkabout" is known as a tough rite of passage, undertaken by indigenous adolescent boys traveling alone and on foot through the bush of the Outback, sometimes for as long a period as six months.

During their walkabout, the young Aborigines trace their ancestors' Dreaming Tracks—pathways marking the route believed to have been taken by creator-beings. There are songs and stories belonging to members of the local tribes and some to the individual boys themselves, explaining the creation of life, people, and animals. The songs, remembered by the young men on their walkabout, enabled them to find the correct route over considerable distances, often through harsh weather and rough walking conditions. The songs describe the terrain that has to be crossed, the much-needed waterholes, and other landmarks.

I saw the movie *Walkabout* in 1971. David Gulpilil, a talented sixteen-year-old indigenous Australian actor and traditional dancer, played the Aborigine boy. The story pictured two white children, abandoned in the bush by their father, meeting the Aborigine boy on his walkabout. The white children, caught up in the young man's journey, were played by Jenny Agutter as the teenage girl and Luc Roeg as her little brother. It was a highly improbable story, but the spectacular outback scenery has stayed with me ever since. In 1985, another movie, *Vision Quest,* referenced the equivalent Native American rite of passage. I have not seen it.

Like the tribal walkabout, the vision quest was intended to provide a turning point in a young man's life. The journey was for self-discovery and to deepen the spirituality of the young men of the tribe. Even today, it is sometimes undertaken by Native American adolescents all alone in the wilderness on a spiritual quest. Eskimos also have their own vision quest, which is said to have an emphasis on sensory deprivation, arduous cross-country walking, lack of sleep and companionship, dire hunger, and other personal challenges.

This is tough stuff. Apart from increased spirituality springing from his aloneness, sheer survival is a major issue for the young man. Often a guardian animal will come to him as a dream or hunger-induced vision. This animal is seen as providing support and help for the youth throughout his life. His journey finally over, the young man returns to his tribe. After the Native American vision quest is completed the boy, now recognized as a young adult, may apprentice with an older man, and eventually will take his place accepted as an adult and sitting with the male elders of the tribe around the evening fire.

Follow your bliss

Associated in my mind with these Hollywood stories, loosely based on real rites of passage, is the attractive teaching on this topic by the famed American mythologist Dr. Joseph Campbell (1904-1987). His famous mantra was: "Follow your bliss and the universe will open doors where there were only walls." Dr. Campbell knew a lot about a variety of rites of passage that he had discovered in ancient societies all over the world, and he approved of their serious purpose. Some may remember in the 1980s, "follow your bliss" became an oft-repeated saying among those who were attracted by the words of kindly Dr. Campbell, who was a gentle but dynamic teacher, popularized in a thought-provoking series on television with Bill Moyers.

Early societies had many different ways of challenging their young men to help them leave childhood behind and become fully adult. It may be that our 21st-century society has substituted wild alternatives, no longer organized by the elders of the tribe but by the adolescents themselves, that serve to replace the older, less hedonist challenges. In the USA they include college societies with fraternities and sororities, binge drinking, sports teams, and marching-band hazing, and college students' notorious unbridled booze-n-sex excesses during the annual spring break.

Adults today have also contributed to the testing of the young by creating sporting contests, and providing young people with some of the challenges in competitive events, from the Olympics down to local sports teams. Physical sports are not without physical danger, and may require intense personal participation for success. In general, however, the majority of today's nuclear families have lost touch with the opportunities that genuine rites of passage once provided in generations past, to give youth a chance to prove itself. So adolescents are tempted to grow fat instead. They immerse themselves in video gaming and texting, hour after hour, and taking little exercise and few social challenges.

In an interview, Winston Churchill bemoaned that "there are not the opportunities that I had." His memory was of fox hunting—a choice that is now very controversial in his native England. Among the young and wealthy in international society today, there comes to mind one big test of manhood—and a lesser but important test of womanhood—involving equestrian activities. Whether it is polo, racing, jumping, rodeo, or the measured world of dressage, a young person's ability to control a horse and succeed in a chosen task is a rough and ready sort of mini-walkabout, it involves young people following their bliss.

Thinking about these practical things, and turning from physical challenges to mental and emotional tests, we note careful preparation by religious organizations of the children and adolescents in their communities to take their due place in the adult fellowship. In Christian churches this usually involves, as its spiritual centerpiece, a promise made by young people to follow in the footsteps of Jesus Christ and a statement of their faith of their "believing in him," in accordance with their church's specific emphasis. Campbell hits the mark here with his saying: "A hero is someone who has given his or her life to something bigger than oneself." [sic]. The Roman Catholic Church's first communion is made at a very young age. Some Protestant churches' historic rite is of "adult" baptism; confessions of faith are made by young people to their bishop; there are formal acts of joining the membership in most if not all churches. Nor should we forget the popular Jewish Bar and Bat Mitzvah. All of these are aspects of this social practice, having to do with carefully crafted plans to retain the enthusiasm of the young, to challenge them to "stand up and be counted" with the faithful, and eventually to give them their place, with adult jobs to do, in the adult community.

In Australia, Aboriginal spirituality is very pronounced. For them the planet Earth is the great parent, giving human life at birth and taking it back again at death. The country in which the tribes dwell is given for men and women to live in for the duration of their lifetime, and is similarly held in sacred trust. The less people take from the Earth, the less has to be returned on their death.

Tribal loyalty reigns supreme, and the dreams and songs of the tribe are shared, providing knowledge of the territory in which the tribe lives. The songs, especially, give the traveler direction in his journey. The young man going on walkabout discovers that the songs he has learned identify his pathway, just as a map would do in a literate society. Providing he keeps to the path identified in the tribal dreamlines and songlines, he will not get into danger by trespassing unwittingly on another tribe's land as he ventures out on his cross-country journey for the test.

The idea of the songline seems to me vitally important in both the Christian church and the Jewish temple, where the idea of using song in their worship of the divine Creator is well established and emotionally motivating and satisfying. Whether an individual church has a cantor, choir, and organ, or the congregation sings in unison without any accompaniment, the fact of singing as a means of gathering together in community is a real point of our contact with the walkabout or vision quest. The power of hymns to teach both doctrine and community togetherness cannot be understated in the spiritual walkabout of modern religious tribes.

Certainly, singing hymns and absorbing spiritual music occupied my young life in the churches we attended. They remain a point of reference to my beginnings as a spiritual human being. The Christian faith was to be found in the hymns I knew, loved, and could and did sing to myself when I was all alone. These days it is the theology that has changed for me. The music constitutes a challenge of a new and rather unwelcome sort. I'd love to sing the music, but I cannot now sing most of the words with acceptance.

Other people point to the liturgy of their church or temple as providing the focal point of their adherence to the faith. Young people may remember gathering in Sunday school, their catechism class, or the youth group in which they played suitable games and learned to dance in the manner approved by the community. Belonging to a church or temple is not just a matter of professing a particular faith, not just learning by rote passages from the sacred scriptures. Rather, it is an amalgam of all the features that attract people and bind them together in community. The process of understanding and belonging to the faith started for me at home, as it did for many of my peers.

Early Days

I grew up in a Christian home in England, my father was a Methodist minister who supplied the Methodist chapels in the Bath Circuit. He also occasionally conducted services in local churches belonging to other denominations. Father was highly regarded as a preacher whose richly illustrated sermons had more in common with a good mystery novel than most heard from the pulpit. He would "divide the Word" of his chosen text by pulling his listeners into the job of puzzling things out for themselves, so that when he reached his conclusion, all had the satisfying sense of having achieved understanding of the biblical passage on their own.

His daily work was in organizing a pioneering non-profit health insurance plan to help the poor when they were sick or when a baby was expected. A truly religious man, he believed that his devotions and prayers should be conducted in the secrecy of his own study. He often quoted the saying of Jesus that we should go into a private room, close the door, and speak to the heavenly Father in secret so that we might be rewarded openly.

Growing up in a minister's household might seem, to people outside the family circle, akin to asking for a daily bath in religion. My parents were liberal Christians, both very convinced of the truth of the gospel. They preferred their faith to be expressed primarily through good deeds and habits rather than religious talk—apart from my father's preaching, of course.

My parents did not engage in reading the Bible with my sister and me in the family setting, as many evangelicals do. They preferred to use various books for their daily devotions, which they chose to tackle in solitude—practicing the presence of God much more than plowing through the Good Book section by section. My memory of any Bible discussion in the family is of my sister, Carrol, who was an intelligent, passionately convinced Christian, bombarding our very own resident minister with theological questions at the dinner table.

My mother, who grew up in a Congregational church family, was a devout woman with a strong belief in the power of prayer. She often quoted Evelyn Underhill, who portrayed prayer as the dominant desire in the human heart. As a Christian, mother was less of a theological conformist than father. She had been interested in the 1920s in the work of Rudolf Steiner and the Theosophists. She had not belonged to any local spiritualist organization, but remained attracted by what they had to say. She would tell me that much, but we never actually discussed the beliefs that had attracted her as a young woman.

Neither of my parents was in any way fundamentalist in attitude toward the Bible. They were not, I believe, entrenched in church doctrine except that of believing in the love of God manifest in the Lord Jesus Christ. Their concern that faith should be a living thing—not a matter of conformity to other people's ideas—was not as much stated in the family as practiced. In consequence, Carrol and I were never enrolled in a Sunday school. Maybe they told Carrol why they had made that decision, but I was left to guess that my parents honestly believed it safer for their children to learn about the faith at home than at the hands of earnest but possibly misguided Sunday school teachers.

The practical result of their policy was that, when the sermon time came in the churches we attended, my nanny or my mother would take me out for a walk, returning in time for the final hymn and benediction. Much nicer than wielding crayons in a silly old

Sunday school! I don't believe my parents ever provided me with any real course of study in the faith to redress the balance. Fortunately, at the schools I attended, teaching in religious education classes and assemblies filled many of the gaps in my knowledge.

It is rather amusing to remember that they positively encouraged my attendance at the youth group of the Argyle Congregational Church we attended during my teenage years. My education had been exclusively in boys' schools from the age of nine. Perhaps Mother thought I needed a little experience of the fair sex. In the youth group leadership was given by a school teacher, Stanley Jones, who was a lifelong pacifist. As I will explain, contact with him resulted in my embracing a pacifist point of view. My parents were very deeply upset at this turn of events. The misguided teaching that they feared the Sunday school might impart had happened in the youth group, despite their desire to keep me safely in the family's Edwardian model..

My spiritual journey—call it "following my bliss" if you prefer Joseph Campbell's name for our personal search for meaning— led me into a wandering walkabout of my own making. I searched my soul long and hard over many years to discover the spiritual basis of my existence, and to find out somewhere a convincing account of what happens to us when our human life is over. The long spiritual search finally made a man of me. I suspect most religiously minded people share the same wandering in a spiritual walkabout, armed no doubt by the dreamlines of Sunday school and the songlines of the hymnbook.

Music

Music was important to my mother, who had a well-rounded artistic talent. She had trained at the Royal Drawing Society in London and had been an art teacher before her marriage. She was also talented musically. Both my parents had occasionally played the piano in church but did not enjoy being picked on to do it. In order to be able to support chapel singing if the pianist failed to turn up, my father had laboriously taught himself how to play hymns on the piano—which he did occasionally with careful, deliberate chords. In a way that was a practical measure of his total commitment to the faith.

Mother played confidently at home from a relatively small selection of lyrical pieces, many of which she had chosen to accompany her fine mezzo-soprano voice. She had an excellent sense of pitch and good musical interpretation. The songs she sang and played were largely classics, but she sometimes included sentimental favorites that were popular in her youth. Occasionally she sang in public at women's meetings held in various Methodist churches, and one year she carried off a rose bowl trophy at the annual Mid-Somerset Music Festival.

I sang along with her joyfully, having a reasonably good soprano voice as a boy, but only a moderate sense of pitch and timing. On one especially memorable occasion I even defeated the high school class leader, Donald James, in the second form's end-of-term results for the music class. That was a big deal for me in those days, because coming "top of the form" in anything was something to which I was not at all accustomed. My chief skill was falling to the bottom of the class.

It could be said that James (we boys used family names when referring to each other) got his own back a few years later. I was slated to play a double-bass solo in the school's annual concert. My piece, called *The Elephant*, was from Saint-Saëns's collection of funny musical sketches, *The Carnival of the Animals*. True to form, I had sadly under-rehearsed myself for the concert, and this time, when music master "Basher" Bennett heard the awful squeaky rumbles I was making, he immediately asked James to conduct a practice session with me.

My classmate, the musical star of the concert and the whole school, played the piano accompaniment over and over again to help me. James was a true musician, destined to teach music later in life, and did not fail to drag me kicking and screaming through the piece until it would pass muster in the concert. That was just as well as my parents were in the audience. I was sweatin', man!

What a mess!

Meeting me today, people see an ancient Brit with a lot of years under his belt, a merry twinkle in his eye, a pun or two on his lips, and a clutch of rotten physical challenges that make him unsteady on his pins and shaky as an aspen leaf. They might rather understandably conclude that this old loon is not a person with much left to say to the world. If they were to look a little deeper, it might become apparent to them that this geezer's life might also be written off as an incredible mess.

Here's a summary of the disaster: When I finished high school I went to Bristol University where I scraped a pass degree in English law but, doubting my commitment to becoming a lawyer, never went on to practice as a barrister or solicitor.

Next, I trained in Birmingham University as a teacher but, in the end, treated teaching as secondary to other occupations rather than as a career, even though one headmaster deemed me good enough to offer me promotion to take charge of the school's religious education department.

While a law student at Bristol, I was quite successful as a Conservative student politician. The Bristol Party organizers suggested that I consider becoming a candidate for the British Parliament, but I ditched genuine political promise in favor of pacifism and resigned abruptly as the student party chairman.

When the time came for my National Service in the military, a government board accepted my plea and deemed me to be a conscientious objector, so I worked as a porter for two years in a London hospital instead. The experience of working with patients persuaded me to ditch a teaching career for the Christian ministry.

Fifteen years after completing theological studies at Cambridge University and being ordained as a Congregational minister, I became so restless theologically concerning the divinity of Christ that I decided to switch denominations and became a Unitarian, entering their British ministry.

I've been married three times: that's really not a good track record. I can imagine Oscar Wilde's Lady Bracknell saying: "To lose one wife is unfortunate. To lose two is *carelessness.*" After the first divorce, from Margaret, I fell in love again, this time to an American by the name of Julie. In consequence I emigrated to the U.S.A., leaving my two kids behind with their mother to fend for them. (There's a *good* daddy!) Margaret remarried, but, sadly, she died soon afterward of breast cancer at the dreadfully early age of forty-eight. That, and not the divorce, was the real tragedy.

For the record, I'm somewhat incompetent with business and money, having dabbled in various sales jobs to make ends meet. In 1980, my friend Bill Billet and I opened a hydraulics spares and equipment outfit, in the middle of a deep recession. The outfit lasted only a few months and led to my bankruptcy. Later, in America, I worked for nearly seven years as a stockbroker. After I retired at the age of 65, I joined Greg Hilton, a great guy with a superb brain, in a little financial consultancy partnership but quit because I did not enjoy the task of drumming up business (nor did he). Are you still reading this? Is this laundry list long enough for you? I'd better stop adding to it before you close the book in disgust.

"So," you ask, "why doesn't this sad old man quietly snuff it and put a quick end to his miserable life?" My answer is simple. On my spiritual walkabout I have acquired something to say that I firmly believe is worth saying. It's what makes me so happy, despite all my switches and failures. It's what makes me genuinely full of good cheer, despite very real physical challenges. It's not something to preach about: my preaching days are over and I have nothing to sell to the world, except my books, of course. It's a meaningful conviction about the nature of the universe, our spiritual nature, the purpose of our life here on Earth, and what happens to us when we die.

What I have to share with you from my walkabout is the great joy I now have in understanding the purpose of life. It grew throughout the tumult of my quest, step by step, year by year, and has finally made a huge difference to my thinking and feeling. It's a difference inside that comes bubbling up for anyone to see. It speaks of a marvelously deep contentment and an understanding of my own self-worth. I'll explain it to you, little by little, as well as I can, so come with me. Really and truly, don't be afraid; this walkabout isn't infectious—and I don't bite!

One thing I understood from my spiritual walkabout is that it must be a journey we each make for ourselves. It takes us from depending as children on the adults in our lives to the point of being fully in charge of our own life. We become determined to be accepted as an adult, and so we must be willing to look after ourselves. It is a passage from the gathering of information in our formal education at school—and by informal finding out what we can about life. Thence to putting into practice what we have learned. It is also, very importantly, a point of departure from meaningless random ideas and feelings to arrive at the place where we have assembled our thoughts sufficiently well to say to ourselves that we truly believe in this or that, and we really will stand up for whatever we hold most dear. We have responsibility for only one life: our own, and for what we do or do not believe.

Looking back on childhood—and mine was a good one as childhoods go—I feel the one thing missing from daily life at home was adequate companionship. My sister and I were treated with love and care, but with more than seven years separating us, we had little to share. There was a loneliness that infected both of our lives and left us somewhat unprepared for the future. It is certain that in general I possessed a better grounding than many other kids in all sorts of ways, but my solitary spiritual walkabout began at an earlier age than was probably the case for some of my peers and has continued for the bulk of my life. It has finally developed into a mature vision of what I am and why I am here. It took time—years and years of time—to be complete and whole inside myself.

Freedom

Wholeness is what the young Aboriginal man on walkabout seeks by the time he returns to his village six months or so after leaving his relatives and his childhood behind. When he set out on his journey it was in order to meet the tribe's requirements for him to mature into a man. He did not really know what he would find in the scrubland of the Outback. The walkabout that we undertake is perhaps less programmed and maybe less insightful than that of the Aborigine, but if we have developed spiritual awareness in the process, it will have been worthwhile. After our life is over, it is our spiritual awareness that will remain to take us to the next outback we are asked to explore.

One of the features of our consumer society is that we are pressured to adopt other peoples' ideas, buy the goods others have to sell, support the causes others have decided to promote, and agree with their belief systems. This book is intended to be different, and if that fails I have only myself to blame. My spiritual walkabout took me away from conformity toward freedom of choice. Freedom is, for me, so important a state of being that I want it to be your experience as well. I will tell the story of my life in brief memoirs and reflections in order to connect with you and your life a bit. The stories show me up—I've really bungled many things. Maybe you have bungled a few—go on, admit it! Hopefully, some of my tales of woe will summon up memories of things you did, ideas you wrestled with, opportunities you won and lost. Let us partner in exploring the outback of our lives so that we may grow wise together.

In the end, I hope you will be open to consider the state where I am now, basically content with my life. I've not got a formula for your success. That will come by your opening up *to yourself* as we go along. There's no gain in becoming a carbon copy of someone else, especially me. We are each in charge of our own life and free to do what our soul tells us. The universe has few rules, but one of the most important is that souls have freedom of choice in all they do. I will explain all that when we get to the right place, but please understand that my intention is to leave you thinking about yourself, your ideas and convictions, not about me and mine. I hope you will like it that way. (Of course there is nothing wrong to mention the book where you got your bright new ideas.)

Mortality and Eternity

When we first come into the world, we have inside our being an immense drive to stay alive. A child who is sick or injured not only expresses its grief very audibly, but fights fiercely to be whole again.

Being full of life is a privilege of the young. There is so much to learn, so much to watch, so much to take part in. As a boy, when the long day was over, I would climb up the 13 steps of the big staircase to the first landing in our home, where I would open the casement window and say in a moderately loud voice (so as to be heard all the way up the garden), "Goodnight, world." No doubt my seniors in the dining room below would chuckle at this nightly ritual. But I knew for sure that in the morning I would be alive, and so would the cat in the yard, the cows on the hill, the bees in the flowers, and all my friends in the natural and human world.

Delight in living is precious. On the other hand, little children find it quite difficult to grasp the meaning of death. Adults are concerned to shield their offspring from the sorrows of the grave if they can. Yet in a sense we only know the fullness of our love of life when we have finally come to grips with the issue of our own mortality. Then, when we have truly assimilated such awareness, we may be ready to take on the spiritual journey during which we will form our opinions and philosophy of life.

Tante

When I was aged about six or so, my great-aunt died. Miss Watson was nicknamed by the family with the French word for aunt, *Tante*. I don't know when this name became attached to her by the family, and I don't remember ever hearing her Christian name. (My mother's side of the family freely played games with personal names: Her father, the captain of a large sailing ship, was always known as "Daddy Bro"; Mother's nickname was "Mume," Father's was "Doe," Carrol's was "Gag," and mine was "Pool.") Anyway, Tante lived at a short walking distance from us in the English city of Bath. She owned a neat little row house stuffed with solid, dark, Victorian furniture and heavy velvet curtains, a decor she reflected in her personal appearance. She was always in a black dress and shawl, with a matching black jade necklace.

My memory of Tante was of someone who was puzzlingly slow and had a wrinkly skin, but who was always very kind to the well-scrubbed little boy in grey school shorts and a little grey blazer with an embroidered school badge sewn onto the top pocket. I had been made fully respectable, with clean hands and nails, curly blond hair sleeked down with water and lots of energetic brushing—a small boy who stood in shocked silence before her magisterial presence. Small boys of six don't mess about in the presence of special people like Tante.

When Tante died, despite my willingness to behave and my youthful curiosity about almost everything, I was deemed too young to go to her funeral. Carrol had seven-and-a-quarter years' seniority, so she went, leaving me to play with my bricks and glass marbles under the watchful eye of our nanny, Nora Irene Woolfitt (nicknamed "Nornie").

Despite that omission, for having been polite and well-scrubbed I inherited one hundred pounds from Tante. It was a goodly sum in those days, and many years later, it bought me a secondhand 1936 Ford 10 motor car that was painted black and was in excellent condition for its age. (Hmm, I wish I was now.) I nicknamed my trusty steed "The Black Prince" and, in one marvelous summer of freedom, drove with my chum Jeff Walker through France, like youthful knights on horseback in a glorious escapade. Come to think of it now, Tante probably would have approved the color of the car. I'll ask her when I get Home.

Most people have tales to tell about their childhood when their grandparents were lost to death. Daddy Bro died when I was a baby; during my childhood the three other grandparents went Home, one after another. I felt some kind of vague connection with them. I liked and respected both my grandmothers but did not feel especially close to either of them. I had not known my grandfather Jenkins very well, but that was to change toward the end of World War II. I visited him for a whole week shortly after Granny Jenkins died. Grandpa was oddly nicknamed "The Boss" behind his back. It was a real misnomer—Granny Jenkins (no nickname!) was the actual driving force of their household.

The Boss

The Boss lived in a little house in Nottingham not far from Wollaton Hall, a spectacular Elizabethan country house. I was then about nine years old and away from home on my own, without my parents for the very first time. My grandfather, a stocky, tough old man, radiated kindness, and he clearly enjoyed seeing his youngest grandchild as much as I liked the novelty of being with him. Grandpa had a glass eye, having had a bad accident once as a toolmaker in a railway workshop. His accident not only cost him his eye but also his job. After the railway company dispensed with his services, he bought a horse and cart and set up shop delivering coal to working-class houses in Saltney, a town in Flintshire, Wales, on the outskirts of Chester. It

17

was a tough, dirty job, which I had observed when the coalmen refilled the coal bunker at our house in Bath.

Despite the problem of low earnings, and through dint of hard work and personal sacrifice, my grandparents had willed, prayed, and pushed their two sons to succeed. My father and Uncle Ernest (nicknamed "Nest") both went to college. Uncle Nest secured a good financial job in the civil service of Nottinghamshire, and father was ordained into the Wesleyan Methodist ministry.

"Would you like to see my glass eye, Peter?"

"Yes, please, Grandpa."

He reached into his eye socket and pulled the glass ball out. It had the image of the eye on one side of it. He told me that it was hand-painted. It was a fair match in color and size with his good remaining eye. I wanted him to hand it to me, but he gently refrained, telling me how it had to be kept very clean. I didn't want to see into his eye socket; the thought made me feel a bit sick. Fortunately he kept his eyelid closed. He secretly slipped the eyeball back into his body and abruptly changed the subject.

"Can you touch your toes?"

We stood opposite each other in the little kitchen. He bent double, touching his toes with ease. Not bad for an eighty-year-old. Truly impressed, I quickly followed suit, just about doing the same—but the glory was all his.

When he died, I thought of my happy week in the presence of the strong little man who continued to smoke his awful pipe in the woodshed at the bottom of the garden, as Granny had insisted when she was alive. He believed that his bacon should be cooked v-e-r-y slowly, so that it did not spoil. He used old-fashioned Paddy soap powder from the local Co-operative Wholesale Society (the "Co-op") to do the washing up—and did a whole list of other delightfully special things my young, observant eyes saw during one of the most loved, most gloriously free weeks of my entire childhood. When he died, I fully understood what that word "died" meant. They all made it abundantly clear that he wasn't coming back. Yet, at the deepest of levels, I did not believe that what they said was really true because my Grandpa, John Henry Jenkins, was very much alive in my heart. He still is, and still I do not weep.

So death was not entirely an academic subject. I had known my grandparents and elderly aunt and had learned that, once dead, they would not re-appear in my daily life. No doubt my parents, nanny, and sister were all pestered with questions. I don't remember doing so, but asking questions was a strong point of mine at that young age.

World War II

Death in the family was not the only experience we had of human mortality. Britain was at war with Hitler's Germany, and death was an everyday topic of people's conversations. It was toward the end of the war when the Nazis' Luftwaffe replaced their much diminished stock of planes with unmanned rockets that they used to bombard the London area. Many people were badly shaken by the random threat of the daily raid by the "doodlebugs," as they were popularly called. My aunt, Dora, suddenly died of a heart attack. I found my mother standing on the top of the wide staircase in our home at Bath, sobbing with grief. Not having been told of what had happened, I displayed some impatience until Carrol took me aside and hissed angrily at me in reasonable concern, "Don't you understand? Mother's lost her sister." I vaguely remember the unkind thought coming into my brotherly mind that I would not be so sad if it were *my* hissing sister who had been lost.

In fact, Dora, the elder daughter, and my mother had been quite close. Their nearly blind mother had shared with them the lonely life of a sailing ship's captain's family. Daddy Bro was away from home not for months but for years at a time. One of my grandfather's more frequent voyages was from Hamburg in Germany to Buenos Aires in Argentina, and from thence round the Cape of Good Hope to catch the trade winds to Australia: first to Perth and then to Sydney or up the coast to Newcastle, New South Wales. Then, making eastward with the prevailing winds round Cape Horn, Daddy Bro's clipper ship would return to the Argentine. The last leg of the journey brought him back at last to the busy port of Hamburg. The management of the shipping line, headquartered at Inverness in Scotland, insisted that captains of the Inver-Line ships remain with their vessels during the cleaning, refitting, and restocking procedures for the next voyage. In consequence, when Captain Watson's little family in Bath received the glad tidings that the *Inveramsey* had docked in the German port, they would hasten to his side, living on the ship for about six weeks until it was time for him to begin another voyage.

As a girl of 17, my mother had sailed with her father as far as Australia, where she visited some relatives, and then returned to Britain on a steamship, via the Suez Canal. The very long voyage left a deep impression on her, and her speech thereafter was daily peppered with seafaring allusions. Dora was less deeply affected by the sea. She was a good sister, wife, and mother, but as the Norris family lived in Harrow, London, for most of the war, she was someone I scarcely knew, so I grieved more for mother in her loss than for Aunty Dora herself. They did not want me to go to the funeral which was quite a long distance away. Carrol went, however. She got to have all the fun, especially funerals.

Going back a little, I remember that I was approaching my fifth birthday when, at about eleven o'clock on 3rd September 1939, we gathered in front of the wireless (as radios were called in those far-off days), which stood on the carved walnut sideboard in the dining room. First came the booming of Big Ben from the clock tower of the Houses of Parliament, then the announcer said importantly, "This is London," and then British Prime Minister Neville Chamberlain announced from the Cabinet Room at 10 Downing Street that Britain and France had just declared war on Hitler's Germany. I sensed my family's anxiety and burst into tears, though I did not know why.

The wireless would bring us wartime news every day of death and destruction both in Britain and in Europe. In general, boys respond positively to the idea of war, and I was no exception, viewing newspaper pictures of the dead and dying, sinking ships, and buildings wrecked by bombs as all being part of normal life—which, of course, they were not. When it came to bombing brick houses with marbles, I was a self-satisfied winner and Herr Hitler always lost.

My parents were pro-war, supporting Mr. Winston Churchill when he took over the leadership of the nation. During the Great War, father had been a wireless operator, tapping signals in Morse code aboard a Royal Navy minesweeper of the Dover Patrol. There wasn't anything more dangerous to do as a job in the Navy than to be guarding the shipping lanes in the heavily mined narrow section of the English Channel between England and France. One day, while my father was off duty on shore leave, he very fortunately missed being blown up by a mine when the boat he had been serving on went down with all hands on board. Even at my young age, I recognized his courage as a seaman, though he made light of his service, for which he had received a medal that he showed me once.

We had remarkably close brushes with death twice in the Bath Blitz—"Blitzkrieg" means "lightning war" in German—when the German Luftwaffe hit the historic City of Bath with high explosives and lots of incendiary bombs. In 1942 there were three attacks on the city between the evening of Saturday 25th April and the early hours of Monday 27th. They caused the death of over 400 of our fellow citizens, and the destruction of, or severe damage to, over 19,000 buildings. My parents, sister, and I twice escaped being numbered among the dead.

At the very beginning of the war we had spent time outside, sheltering with our neighbors the Coleborns in a cold, covered trench next door when the air raid sirens went off. Then, as the war dragged on, we changed course; the four of us gathered as a family, whenever the wailing alarm sounded, in my father's study. It was deemed to be the safest room in the house. We were there on the first day of the Bath air raids. Father, who was wearing his Air Raid Warden's helmet, nipped out to stand in the large front doorway of our house, smoking his pipe and watching the fires burn in the valley of the river Avon, quite a long way from where we lived.

We had by then become fairly used to the drone of enemy planes going overhead on their way to bomb and strafe (attack with gunfire) targets in the industrial centers of South Wales, the Midlands of England and the nearby port city of Bristol. The people there had a very bad time, though not nearly as bad as the hard-hit Londoners. German planes, each one decorated with the heavy black Iron Cross on either side of their fuselage, would sometimes off-load the odd bomb or two on Bath, on their way back to France.

It was different this time, Father reported. Bath was clearly the Nazis' target. He could see the bombers were going after the London-to-South-Wales railway lines and possibly, if they could find them, the various sites of the headquarters of the Admiralty, which had been moved well out of London to Bath where they controlled the operations and supply of the British Navy.

Father came in and we settled down to sit out the raid. Then we heard the sound of two or three aircraft flying in from the south, close above the rooftops. There was a huge noise: a heavy thump followed by a very big explosion. I felt the large chair I was sitting in jump an inch or two into the air. Then came a great crashing and rattling sound, as debris from the back garden of the house three doors away poured directly onto our roof. By the cold light of dawn we discovered that the nearby neighbors' house, where the bomb had fallen, was badly shaken but not destroyed. The force of the explosion had lifted rocks and dirt from the garden where it went off, high into the air and clear over the two neighboring houses, to fall directly on ours. My parents were very annoyed at being singled out in that way. Interestingly, though, that bomb unearthed an empty Roman stone coffin, without a lid—or any bones. An expensive archeological dig, one might say. The Romans had the practice of burying their people beside the main roads. A few years later, while digging at the top of our back garden, I discovered a yard or two of stones set in a kind of pavement, but I covered it up again for someone else to discover. It could have been part of the Fossway, a Roman road.

Next night, my father arranged a "safe" venue for us. He was a member of the Bath city council, and worked on committees with the Chief Medical Officer of Health for Bath, whose family home was among the green fields of Claverton Down, located well away from the city's suburbs. Mother agreed that we would be safe there. After he had driven us to his friends' house, we watched Father go off to his civil defense duty in town. His principal war service in WWII was as a duty officer in the city's central command, where they directed the ambulances and rescue services.

When Father returned the next day, he had a tale to tell of how his team had been working the phones in the basement of the headquarters' house when it was hit by a bomb. They had been flung across the room by the blast, but all the members of the team were able to pick themselves up and continue telephoning. Happily the telephone bank not been affected by the explosion, but part of the old building, a decorative tower, was totally destroyed.

Not to be outdone by him, we had our own story. Shortly after arriving at the place of refuge, Mother, Carrol, and I were treated by our hostess to a tour of some of the features of her lovely home. We had just entered the large dining room when a lone German plane suddenly roared overhead, coming very low above the ground. Immediately, we heard the whistle of bombs dropping. It had released a stick of six devices in all—three falling at the back and three in front of the house. The bomb blasts were accompanied by gunfire. One bomb exploded on the back lawn just outside the room where we were standing. The glass of the windows in the room was punched in by the blast, carrying the heavy velvet curtains like a bizarre moving wall of destruction. Both glass and curtains came halfway toward us through the air before crashing down on the dining table. The velvet was cut to ribbons, but the glass had no force left when some of it reached us. We had escaped again without even a scratch, but it was a very near thing. Had it been dropped only a few feet closer we would all have died that night..

Probably I should have got a clear message from these experiences, but despite bombs and coffins, death was not on my radar. I had been very close to being killed, but I considered it to be all part of the job of living; it had not rattled my youthful psyche seriously. That was still to come.

Trouble

As it was, my desire was to live life to the full. I was quite capable of getting into trouble. The list of my crimes and misdemeanors was a long one. I threw gravel at another schoolboy in an argument. All hell was then let loose. I was sentenced before the whole school not to wear to school my green school cap with a badge, for the eternity of a whole month! My mother stoutly defended my need of warm headgear and provided a plain brown cap that quickly became the envy of my peers. As part of the adult settlement, my father promised to make me do gardening as a punishment. When it came to Saturday we went out into the garden, and after only five minutes of my raking grass he let me go. Perhaps he had thrown gravel at someone when he was a lad.

Conscience still troubles me about another incident. From the upstairs landing at a friend's house, I poured the bathroom cleanser Harpic into the face of my pal. I would surely have been killed by his mother had she known, but the boy said it tasted sweet and I swore blind that I had used a pack of sugar that I had in my pocket. Harpic was then advertized to go "clean round the bend" of toilets. In truth it was I who had gone round the bend—crazy kid. That was a lesson to me, and I never did something like that again.

Lying is an issue with every child born. Imaginative kids who grow up to write stories and memoirs when they are old are the sort of wild animal that gets into lots of trouble with truthfulness—or rather, the lack of it. Despite that, today I only remember one other really deliberate lie. I stole a cigarette from my mother's opened box, and then earnestly suggested to my parents that perhaps the manufacturers had only packed 19 instead of 20 in it. Astonishingly, my parents accepted my argument at face value, and mother said she would write to the makers. I crawled away to my room to agonize over the dreadful lie that I had told. My mother never wrote to the company. Instead she decided that her very occasional cigarette was a bad example to me, so she gave up smoking at once. I didn't follow that lead, alas. Have you ever tried smoking dried lilac flowers? Don't!

I was still too young to have developed what evangelicals call "a consciousness of sin." That came later in my life, as I growingly adopted a religious point of view. By my early adolescence I had acquired an understanding of two things that the church treated as important. The message was carefully conveyed to my young brain. The first was the perfect example of Jesus Christ. Gravel, Harpic, cigarettes, and lies were not things that Jesus would ever have got mixed up in. He was a *good* man. He cared, as my father cared, for the poor, the lost, and even for young gravel and Harpic throwers. The perfection of Christ was not a phrase I would have used, but the concept was placed firmly in my mind. The Christmas carol, Once in Royal David's city says it plainly:

> "Christian childen all must be,
> Mild, obedient, good as He."

This was the spiritual conviction that forgiveness was something Jesus was jolly good at.. Jesus would not have beaten me *really hard* as my mother did one morning when I accidentally broke her alarm clock. (Don't worry, I've forgiven her.) My guess is she had been saving up that drubbing for months.

Samuel

The second thing the church managed to convey to me was that God was going to call me into His service. Of all the messages of the faith, this was the one it most successfully imparted. The story of the little acolyte Samuel in the temple was the key to this major ecclesiastical success. One night, hearing a strange voice calling out, "Samuel, Samuel" and seeing no one, the little lad was puzzled. He trotted off to the old priest Eli, who was having a snooze. On the third occasion of the voice calling and little Sammy trotting off again to pester Eli, the sleepy old guy woke up to the crystal clear religious significance of the event—it had happened *three* times—and told the lad that if and when he heard the voice of God again, he should respond by saying that he was all ears and would listen. (And please tell Eli all about it tomorrow because he *really* needs to sleep *now*.)

I waited for a voice to call me, of course. It was a long wait. In the end it became clear that the positive feelings that we usually call intuition are our so-called "inner voice." I also came to realize that the thing we claim is our "call" bubbles up in our heart, and bypasses our ears. But, nevertheless, the concept of a call has remained something I even now hold dear.

It was many years after my first hearing of the Samuel story that I had a remarkable personal spiritual experience. By this time, about 1970, I was minister of a Congregational church in Wimbledon, London. It was a busy life because I was teaching full time in the Wandsworth Boys' School in order to support my ministry financially. The church was quite poor, but it provided a nice, rent-free house.

I was attending some church conference or other. I have little memory of where it was or what it was about, but my guess is it was at a large country house north of London. The conference center had a converted barn as a meeting room that we had used that first evening for Bible study and prayers. Then the conference attendees had all walked down the hill to the center for an evening drink of hot chocolate before going to bed. I was left alone at the barn door.

Life had been rather tough of late, and I was facing issues, now long-forgotten, that had made me somewhat depressed. I walked back into the barn to pray. No one else was there. Suddenly a great sense of an immensely powerful presence swept over me. I fell to my knees and, believing that I was in the presence of the Holy One, whispered Samuel's refrain: "Speak, for your servant hears." There was a long pause. The powerful feeling ebbed away, leaving me totally convinced that I had been visited by—Someone.

The difficulty of pinpointing who or what had come into my life was baffling. It seemed to be divine and powerful, yet it was dumb and left no discernible message except, perhaps, that it had been there for me and me alone. I talked about it to a friend, the composer and entertainer Donald Swan, with whom I had just been involved the week before in a BBC TV religious broadcast. Next thing I knew, a recorded account of the experience was being discussed by a panel of experts, including Donald. They appeared to conclude in a kindly way that it had been linked with my feeling somewhat depressed. I failed to feel that their conclusion made any sense of my experience, but I still did not know what it was.

Fast-forward twenty years (I've got lots and lots of years to play with!) and you will find me alone in the one-room apartment in the heart of Indianapolis, USA, that I had rented when first employed by Charles Schwab & Co. as a stockbroker. Much had happened to me recently. My second wife Julie and I had separated, and I had finally brought the curtain down on my ministry. Now I was in a new job that I did not know much about, and certainly had not by then started to enjoy. It was Saturday evening when I had been trying to meditate in the gathering gloom, the room lit by distant street lights.

After a while of being silent and empty of thought, I entered into an awareness that is hard to describe except with the words that made sense at the time. There was a presence, a benign presence in the room, loving me gently but not overpowering me. I felt no desire to say that I would listen to what it might have to say to me. The reason was partly that I felt joined to it, one with it. Partly it was that the experience could only be described as a feeling of infinity—gentle, loving, supportive infinity.

This time there was no panel of experts discussing my experience on the television. It was the last such feeling I have had. It remains an enormously emotive incident in my memory. On neither occasion could I truly identify at the time who or what it was that had happened to me. I can hazard a guess these days, now I claim to be a little more enlightened, and now believe that it was an experience of meeting directly with my eternal soul. We will explore that concept more thoroughly in a while.

When people see visions, hear voices, feel presences, or have near-death experiences, most of them never tell anything to anyone about what has happened to them. We feel strongly that something very intimate and precious has happened to us. Generally speaking we don't find it easy to identify what exactly took place. All we know is that we want to safeguard the feeling lest a doubting Thomas get hold of our story and ridicule us. There is a general agreement by commentators on people who have had near-death experiences: They usually don't want to talk to other people about it, but their subsequent lives are often radically changed for the better. I am sympathetic with those who cannot bring themselves to accept the reality of what is broadly called "spiritual" ideas and experiences. My best response is to say that all I know is what it happened to me: interpret it if you like. Take it or leave it and if it so happens that the experience has been a good one, helpful in your life then relish it.

Danger and Death

Vehicles of all shapes and sizes have nearly been my downfall on many occasions. The first was the familiar child's trolley called a "Radio Flyer." It was quite stoutly built, largely wooden with metal trim, and had been imported from America before World War II. My parents bought nearly all my toys secondhand during the war. This simple, four-wheeled wagon with a long steering handle has been manufactured by a company of the same name since 1917, and is still going gangbusters today. I had a lot of fun with it as a little kid.

Westmead, the house where I grew up, was large and built of Bath stone mined in the nearby oolitic limestone quarries. It was constructed in 1912, as the large inscribed date on the front of the house solemnly proclaimed. My parents purchased it from a Greek shipping magnate at a heavily discounted price, because the owner was dumping it on the market during the Great Depression. Mother had inherited a handy sum of money in the form of an investment in Argentinean railways from her uncle Arthur, who had been a seafaring captain like Daddy Bro. He had retired from the sea early and had bought a ranch in Argentina, near Buenos Aires, prospering mightily and amassing a genuine fortune. In addition to the house, his legacy enabled my parents to buy lovely antique furniture during the war when prices were very low. But nearly all of the investment was lost when the Argentine government nationalized their railways during the war, and a valuable collection of family jewelry was snatched by burglars one day when we were all out somewhere.

Back to my game: There was a gentle slope on the garden path around the big house from the back yard to the terrace in the front. With a suitable push of the Radio Flyer wagon, resembling the start of an Olympic bobsleigh ride, I was able to get up just enough momentum to take me round the southeast corner of the house, past the side bay of the drawing room, turning at the northeast corner sharply to avoid plunging down the front steps leading to a sloping orange-brown gravel path and the main road. Then, if my momentum was correctly assessed, flyer and boy went gliding along the front terrace of the house and even just around the northwest corner—if really lucky. The main goal of my circular ride was to get around that third corner. As time went on, I had become more skilled at getting there, but it demanded a fast start and very careful steering with the long arm of the tiller that controlled the front wheels. As a childhood lesson in goal-setting, that heady ride was tops.

Another fine, warm day dawned for my "trolleying." With a good run to start off, I scrambled aboard the little truck as it rounded the first corner, my hand firmly on the tiller. This time, wanting to get as wide an arc as possiblr in the ride around the northeast corner of the house, I steered too close to the stone boundary wall, scraping my hand hurtfully. The sudden pain caused me to jerk the tiller in the wrong direction as I came to the top of the garden steps. Down the first three steps flew the Radio Flyer trolley with me hanging on for life, then along the flat before the next similar drop. How I remained upright in the cart is hard to say. Bouncing down the last three steps added greatly to the Flyer's momentum. All that was left was the gravel path and the half-open garden gates—then I would be out on the main road, unable to stop. Luckily the gravel slowed down the wagon's headlong rush. It crashed into the garden gate, spilling me out on the stony path just as the double-decker bus roared past.

My love affair with the trolley was at an end. Picking myself up and removing bits of gravel from my face, knees, and clothes, my chief desire was to hide what I had done from my mother. I might well have died going down the steps or sliding into the road under the bus. But that is an adult afterthought and it was never truly in my mind. What made me anxious was the thought of being given another "good talking to," as mother called disciplinary agony sessions, for acting dangerously and scraping my hand so badly.

The incidence of children falling off their sledges and tin trays, when sliding down snow-covered slopes, is too common to merit much mention, although you may have a harrowing tale of your own to remember. There was a wicked slope on the fields behind Westmead that was chosen by the local boys for sledding. In fact my little friends, a majority of whom were girls, chose slopes farther along the hillside that were not so dreadfully steep. My parents had bought a "proper" adult sledge at an auction sale to give me one Christmas. It stood high above the snow, its thin metal skids supported by stout pillars. Fortunately, we kids did not think of racing. It was every girl for herself (plus me). We would toil up the hill, get on our sledge or tray, slide down, and then repeat the climb. My new sledge went farther than the others, however. How I avoided death crashing into one of the many trees at the bottom of the field I will never know. Childhood is full of such dangers and of miraculous escapes.

Death was an occasional topic in the family's dinnertime conversations. Father would be moved sometimes to read out from the newspaper a name or two of notable people who had died, and to comment briefly on the loss of life in the war, but the emphasis was not on the meaning of death. Death was simply "a fact of life" in wartime.

Only in one respect do I remember Father waxing really eloquent about death. Somehow, one dinnertime, the topic of Agatha Christie's mystery novels came up—with a dead body in the library and another in the garden. Father uncharacteristically did not approve of such books. He was not given to suggest censorship, even when *Lady Chatterley's Lover* was hotly debated in Britain. For him, however, death was too serious a matter to be the basis of a novel in that way. He did not disapprove of the skill of the novelist, just the idea of basing a story on the death of a human being. That cheapened life for the readers, he said. I believe that at the back of his mind Father felt he was witnessing the lowering of social standards in many ways. This was for him yet another example of that decline.

Argyle

One of the consequences of the war concerned the central New King Street Methodist chapel, which we attended. It had been bombed to bits in the 1942 Bath blitz. Its congregation was temporarily moved to the undamaged central Congregational churh in Argyle Street, Bath. My mother had been raised in the nearby historic Percy Congregational Church, which had also been hit badly in the same firestorm. So our family, with my father, whenever he was not preaching somewhere, settled into a pew on the right-hand side of the church, the end of which featured the congregation's First World War memorial on the wall in wood and brass. I used to look up at the names inscribed there and wonder what it must have been like to be a soldier in those days. Mother chose the pew, I guess, because the memorial listed the sacred name of her fiancé, who had been killed in France—at the battle of the Somme, I believe.

The days rolled on. I grew bigger and stronger and now was a gentle youngster of 15 summers, quite tall for my age but not physically as tough as I would like. I wasn't thrilled by doing push-ups and weight lifting—gardening was my chosen way of developing muscles—but one fateful day in 1950, the muscle power I needed was in my head and not in my brawny arms.

Robin

A little scarlet-feathered robin redbreast was searching for earthworms and grubs in the patch of ground I was digging. The agile bird was so fearless that it was hopping about a little more than a spade's length away from me. It had done so before and was a true companion. The ground was heavy to work, with lots of roots. At mother's request, I was going to plant red currant bushes in the gently sloping garden, just above the greenhouse where we grew tomatoes and cactus plants with prickles that came off easily and remained in your skin for ages.

Despite the cool of the English autumn day, I was hot and tired. Pausing from work, I went to lean my back against the greenhouse doorpost. My friend the robin hopped on my spade, stuck upright in the ground, and proceeded to preen its little wing feathers and beautiful red breast. I can see him now.

I had taken up the garden with me a small air pistol that my father had recently allowed me the freedom to use all by myself. This was my second or third day out shooting with it. That morning I had spent a busy time in the lower garden, targeting a rusty old tin can placed on a post at a reasonable distance. It was more fun doing hard shots than easy, so I had been running when shooting—and missing, of course.

Watching the robin, I idly picked up the pistol from the shelf of the greenhouse and loaded it with a pellet, intending to shoot at the deserted pen in which we had housed Khaki Campbell ducks during the war. Suddenly the robin lifted off from the spade and alighted on the branch of a black currant bush immediately in front of me. Unthinking, I gripped the pistol, pulled the trigger, and fired at the bird. My innocent friend the robin tumbled down and rolled onto its back on the ground, with its little feet in the air. It did not stir because it was quite dead.

At first I could not even grasp what had happened. I had not intended to shoot at any living thing—let alone my little feathered companion, Mr. Robin Redbreast. It was stunning to see the poor wee thing who had been the star of the show only a few minutes before, lying there in death. I was left gasping for breath, with tears starting from my eyes in a veritable flood. I was a murderer and my lethal weapon was still in my hand. Guilt and shame consumed my heart, and a fearful desire for secrecy swept over me lest anybody should ever know about the awful deed I had just done. In that regard I have not been true to that intention and have told the tale to others before now, once or twice even from the pulpit.

This is a memory that I do not cherish, of course, but one that had a hand in shaping my life from that dreadful day forward. Robin did not deserve to die at the hand of a thoughtless teenager, but the gift he gave me in dying was immense. Even as I buried the little carcass in a grave marked by stones and watered with my tears, I knew that something vitally important had just happened to me.

Eventually, having finished my sorrowful digging, I planted the bushes, watered them in, and walked slowly back to my home down the long garden with its many plum, apple, and pear trees. Going into the big house, shaken and sad, I made for the study and left the pistol on my father's desk for him to put away again in the locked cupboard in his bedroom. Although human death had already occurred in my life, my senseless slaughter of Robin still ranks as the most important milestone in my process of coming to terms with the fact of physical death. From then on I had a small quantity of emotional pain to justify my quest for meaning in life, and to evaluate the bliss that one day I would follow.

Hormones

In the five years that followed the Robin incident, my awareness of the possibilities of life became much more acute. We leave childhood by degrees, taking a little step here, for example, in our relationships with family members; and a little step there, for example, in our thinking about religion. "Argyle," as we called the church, had become the family's regular place of worship after the Blitz took away the central Methodist church. From then on I grew up in the Congregational church, went to their youth club, joined the congregation as a member on profession of faith, and eventually became a Congregational minister. It was a church walkabout that worked fairly well in my life... for a time.

The adolescent is often seen as excessively hormonal, and boys of 14 to 20 are thought of today as driven by their sexual urges. But the development of my sexuality was a slow one. Having been educated in boys-only schools from the age of nine, I was more attracted by the courtly language of the Elizabethan lyrical poets than by real live girls. I joined the youth group at church when I was about 16. Several of my school friends were in the mix there. We enjoyed watching the girls playing table tennis, girls playing snooker, girls dancing folk and square dances, and, of course, as the highlight of the evening, we relished walking girls home. There were also outings to the country we went on together and a youth conference after Christmas.

Teenage hormones sometimes involved a lot of actual walking. When I was about 19, I was hungrily chasing the beautiful Jane, whom I had met in the Sunday afternoon youth study group. On my first day there, she had sat in front of me, her hair brushed neatly into a gorgeous long pigtail. Jane was a popular, lively girl, and I was astonished at my good luck when she agreed to let me walk her home to Weston, the Bath suburb where she lived. Walking somebody home from youth club was serious business, but there were very well-understood rules of conduct: the reward for such chivalry was kissing—nothing more (so far as I knew). After kissing each other behind the garden hedge so that her parents would not see (but they did), she went inside, and I was left to find my way home, speed-walking, jogging, and sometimes even desperately running across the city, trying to get home by mother's deadline hour.

One winter, the youth group went on a church-run weekend conference that was devoted to Bible study, discussion, games, and, less officially, more kissing. The conference was situated in the little village of Monkton Combe ("coom"), to the south of Bath, at a boys' boarding school that was closed for the Christmas "hols." The girls were assigned individual bedrooms in one of the houses, and the boys had beds in a dorm room in another—with the eagle-eyed youth leader, Jean, making sure that at nightfall this separation of the sexes would stay that way. However, there was no accounting for hormones, mine in particular!

If there had been any signs that Jane was falling for someone else, I had not twigged them. I was dimly aware that my friend I'll call "Jim" was seeking her attention, but pride kept me from facing up to basic facts—their holding hands and whispering secrets, for example. Earlier in the day, Jane had pointed out to me her solo bedroom on the top floor, which featured a dormer window in the roof, looking out on the school's central courtyard. That evening, after the conference members had gone their several ways to bed, I went alone into the courtyard and hungrily surveyed the girls' building opposite. Jane's window was lit and it beckoned to me like a lighthouse to a drowning sailor.

Directly down from the dormer was a drainpipe. It channeled water from the heavy cast iron guttering past one set of windows to the tall ground-floor classrooms, and then discharged its contents into an open drain. Floating on a sea of hormones I said to myself, "I'll do it." Grasping the drainpipe firmly I began to climb.

When I hear sad tales of teenagers who have been killed in car accidents, I remember precisely what it was like to feel invincible. Death is not a reality to most teens, and their minds give its presence no credence. Dying is something that other people do. We feel it has no meaning that we can apply to our young lives. It was with the same absence of reflective thought with which I had killed Robin that I climbed the drainpipe that night. It was far from easy to do, much harder than climbing the rope in the school gym had ever been. I gave no thought to the risk of pulling the pipe out of the wall with my weight and continued on up, past the second set of windows. Then came the roof's wide overhang: I still have no idea how I ever mastered that obstacle, only that I knew then, in my now terrified and shaking body, that I would be quite unable to climb back down again.

So I scrambled up the rest of the roof and tapped on the window. Jane came and opened the window and helped me in, but then I knew the awful truth. Through a gap in the curtains I had seen Jane sitting on my rival's knees, kissing him—like crazy. Later, he and I crept out of the building together and avoided being caught by Jean. I never apologized to them for spoiling their fun. Having become aware of how much I had risked that night, I wasn't in the mood. Last time I saw Jane she was married a youth group friend, and they were living happily ever after.

Maggie

In my story is a bittersweet memory. Margaret was also a member of the Argyle youth group. Folk dancing, as I have said, was a feature of our program, and "Maggie" patiently taught me the little-known dance called the "Moonlight Saunter." We walked home from Argyle from time to time (walking briskly in the moonlight), and later, after several years of just sending each other Christmas cards, we met, fell in love, and were married in Argyle by the minister, the Rev. Jack Coggan, on the day of the Winter Solstice, 1962. An absent friend from our youth group days sent a teasing telegram: "How wise of you to choose the shortest day." Margaret bore our two wonderful children, Hazel and Jonathan. She was a sweet, loving person who shared many of my convictions and gave me consistent support. She was a fine nurse with a great track record at the Westminster Hospital, London, where she trained, and much later as the much-loved Matron of the Bristol Old People's Welfare's geriatric nursing home. But, far too young, she died courageously, after a long fight with breast cancer. She did not deserve the dreadful husband (me) that she got first time around.

Double yellow lines

At last, in old age, I have become more cautious with running risks. But following my childish inability to register fully the possibility of death while playing with the Radio Flyer, and after nearly crashing the high-class sledge, and—the worst—during my teenage drainpipe climbing escapade, I did at last come to a mental understanding. Yet for years afterward, my ability to defy obvious danger continued unabated as I drove on the always dangerous highways and byways of Britain.

I still have to close my eyes and breathe deeply when I remember bringing my pre-war 350cc Matchless motorcycle to a fast stop at a "zebra" pedestrian crossing in Saltford, a little town that I traversed daily on my way to Bristol University. The heavy truck right behind me skidded to a halt on the wet road, a hairsbreadth away from my back wheel. The truck driver discovered within the depths of his magnificent being a rich supply of colorful language with which to entertain me. The aged pedestrian who had been waiting to cross the road disappeared in a puff of purple smoke and must have been an angel—just kidding!

Shortly after that event, the British adopted double yellow lines on dangerous bends of major highways. Then I was at one with the worst of them, overtaking slower drivers—those idiots who honked their miserable antiquated horns, yelled cleverly crafted medieval oaths, and used inappropriate hand signals when I overtook them on double yellow lines. This contributed to my youthful denial of danger until, one day, my rear-view mirror filled with beautiful flashing colored lights, accompanied by vigorous, heavy-duty goose-like raucous honking.

The magnanimous and good looking policeman, who took my personal details lovingly, sweetly volunteered that he would not report me for dangerous driving as, rather unfortunately, that would certainly result in my license being suspended—a pity since I had no previous convictions. Instead, he would book me with the lesser charge of "driving without due care and attention," which only carried a stiff fine. Swallowing my pride, I mailed the fine (ouch!), realizing I had got off lightly, thanks to his noble consideration. The constable deserved a knighthood. My driving improved but remained true to form. Death still wasn't an issue for me, only for other people.

Muffy

Fast-forwarding to middle age, I will inevitably cause many readers' hearts to beat sadly with personal grief remembered in recalling the euthanasia of our gentle, sweet-tempered family cat, Muffy. She was old and in obvious pain. Margaret and I decided that it would be kinder for her to be "put to sleep" than to live out the rest of her days in pain. Note the phrase used in place of a term that some might consider too unpleasant. People sanitize death with euphemisms such as "put to sleep." We also ascribe the decision to take an animal's life to our own kindness and thoughtfulness, regardless of whether it also happens to bring to an end the practical difficulties and expense we have shouldered in caring for our pet—a burden for its human family that would be lifted by the pet's passing.

I was the one chosen to take Muffy to the animal hospital, where a small injection finished her earthly feline life and a donation ensured that we would not be required to bury her body. All felt very straightforward and satisfactory until I got into the car and put the empty cat carrier on the seat beside me. Now Muffy was not there, and the absence of her sweet energy was palpable. Despite all the best reasons that we could muster, the fact of the matter was that my wife and I had conspired to murder her. Having stopped my car at the side of the road for safety's sake, I let the waterworks flow. In my thoughts, Robin was there as well, with his little feet in the air. To you it may seem unfeeling of me, but I have probably grieved more over their deaths than I ever have for any human being. Maybe my instinct was telling me a truth that my conscious mind could not yet fully grasp: animals die—do we?

Cousins

When, years later, my cousin Malcolm Norris died suddenly at the early age of 64, his life as a university administrator and students' guru was at full flood. There was a tremendous outpouring of grief by colleagues and students, as well as within our family. By this time I had emigrated to America. I made the difficult choice not to take leave of absence from my work and fly across the Atlantic to attend the funeral.

Malcolm, who was three-plus years older than I, had dazzled me as a boy when he came to Bath with Harry, his equally interesting, wonderfully kind elder brother. On one glorious visit, Malcolm was passionately into Shakespeare, specifically his play *Henry V*. There was talk of Laurence Olivier's recent Technicolor movie, of armor and weaponry, of pig-faced bassinets (a type of helmet), and of heraldic armorial bearings. Malcolm had a hearty chuckle that I tried to imitate afterward, and an ability to sketch funny cartoons, which I never could emulate.

I reeled away in happiness after his visit to raid the Bath municipal library of books on the battle of Agincourt. I saw the film of *Henry V*, of course, and learned some of Henry's speeches by heart. Malcolm went on, as a young man, to make rubbings on rolls of paper of all the monumental church brasses in the entire kingdom. He published *Monumental Brasses*, still the definitive book on the subject, and several other volumes, including one on commemorative memorial brasses in Germany. My heart still aches to hear the whole story of his exceptional life.

Cousin Harry and I met from time to time, when I was living in London, at Lyons Corner House, Trafalgar Square, for tea and a chat which I greatly enjoyed. He had been in the British intelligence service during the war and spent his time in North Africa among the Bedouin people. He taught colloquial Arabic in London University after the war, and was always telling us in his letters of faraway places he had visited to give a lecture. I knew Harry and Malcolm as the best of boys and the best of men.

Malcolm's sudden and early demise represented for me a personal engagement with death on a deeper level—somewhat akin to the deaths of my parents. But, strong as my emotional response was at their passing, there was an element missing from each of the three experiences that made them all different from the demise of Robin and Muffy. Of course, you might well conclude that the difference was that I was complicit in the death of both the bird and the cat. You might say I had a bad conscience, which sharpened grief with the whetstone of guilt. But that was not it. I believed when Malcolm died, and my 85-year-old and senile mother died, and my father, ripened to perfection, passed on at the age of 93, that their deaths were not a real end to them. I would be with them again. I could not say that about my little non-human friends—despite my hopes. There may be some who will conclude my attitude to death was simply a psychological flaw, and means nothing more than that I'm an unthinking and heartless fellow who does not deserve support in his latter days as a sick old man. I don't think they are correct. Maybe what I have written makes sense to you from your own experiences.

As an aside, I have been fascinated by an incredible sharpness in the pictures that come back to me as I retell the Robin and Muffy stories. I see the pots with cactus plants in them sitting on the shelf of the greenhouse where I was standing when I fired the air pistol at Robin. The cat carrier on the passenger seat of the family car without our beloved cat, is remembered with an accuracy that I could draw in detail - were I artistically gifted. Grief has locked the pictures so that I cannot forget them.

Doubts and Certainties

The Reverend Jack Coggan, minister at Argyle for many years, was something of a hero in the eyes of the young people of the church youth group. He was tolerant and supportive, he knew how to make us laugh during his sermons, and he kept out of the way of our youthful antics. When he finally left the pastorate, the denomination promoted him to be a Moderator, our church denomination's spiritual equivalent of bishop in other churches, but with little temporal power.

I had just started my law studies at Bristol University when Mr. Coggan announced a series of sermons he called "Christian Certainties." I was more than ready to listen. The church was important to me, and I looked up to him. Moreover, Professor Coutts, the law faculty Dean, whose subject was Jurisprudence (legal theory), was a sharp critic of Christianity, especially Roman Catholicism, and mounted the most serious challenge to religious faith that I had ever encountered in my life so far. Most of my fellow law students had been through one of the church-based instruction programs, and the professor's attacks on religion drew them into heated debates with him, which I listened to but in which I did not choose to take an active part.

Coggan vs. Coutts

Without either of them knowing, the minister was pitched against the law professor in my mind. I listened carefully to each. I tried to match what I was hearing, although in truth much of what each said did not directly answer the other. Coutts talked constantly about "ratiocination, or reasoning" (an oft-repeated phrase that reduced us students to major giggles). He put forward a clear case that in our thinking about law, morality, justice, and religion, we had to be careful not to let unverifiable ideas cloud our vision of the truth. Coggan talked the language of a reasonable faith. He put forward a carefully crafted list of those ideas upon which the Christian mind might safely depend. It was an intelligent and able presentation, worthy of a fine preacher. My mother and sister, who heard the whole series, were much impressed.

Coutts had fired the opening salvos of the battle for my mind. After a while I told my fellow students at Bristol that I was an agnostic. I still went to the youth group at Argyle, where there were friends from school to mingle with—and girls to kiss, so long as you didn't actually call yourself agnostic. I suppose it gave one bad breath.

Many would say that my flirting with the agnosticism of the law professor was part of a youthful rebellion. It is true that I rebelled against aspects of my life at home, but I don't think my agnosticism was essentially a rebellion. It was an awakening to the feeling that I had freedom to think for myself. In fact I never really liked Coutts's sharp way of reasoning. If the battle for my mind had been assessed on the basis of personality, Coggan would have won hands down. What had happened to me was a genuine walkabout experience: I had discovered a piece of my manhood. It was an intellectual something, and as things worked out, my change of heart was short-lived. Yet, in another sense, Professor Coutts's victory over Reverend Coggan has stayed with me as a permanent feature of my thought process. I bring my homemade version of "ratiocination, or reasoning" (damn you, Coutts) to matters of enquiry and belief. It has made it impossible to call ideas "certainties," Christian or otherwise, while there are doubts in my mind.

Evangelism

Next came what turned out to be only a minor blip on the religion scene. The evangelist Billy Graham had set up shop in the old greyhound racing track, Harringay Arena, for his first London Crusade in March 1954. Evangelical churches in Bath booked the Pavilion, Bath, a large hall where some of my mates went roller skating and practicing their kissing on Saturday nights. The youth group decided by popular vote to go en masse to experience "Modern American Evangelism" as one leaflet called the crusade.

There was a good deal of excitement, not just among evangelicals. Liberal churches, which did not usually go in for evangelical appeals, woke up to the idea that they should not miss out in bringing people to Christ. Jack Coggan himself conducted a somewhat evangelical service, and a few people walked up to the front to acknowledge Jesus Christ as their Lord and Savior. I did not stir from my pew. Neither my parents nor my sister had turned up at the well-advertised service. Although Father had been raised in an evangelical tradition, he did not feel a need to be present. I sense that the big failure of Billy Graham's message for me was his inability to engender in me a "consciousness of sin," a feeling of personal need that provides the basis of the evangelist's good news that Jesus died for our sins and we may be "washed in the blood of the Lord.".

Nothing changed in my life because of Billy Graham. Most of the youth group went to the Pavilion service and emerged unscathed, somewhat amused by the organizers' serious tone, and were very put off by their forceful appeal for money. I continued in my double life as agnostic at Bristol and churchgoer at Argyle.

The change that would come soon was to be a positive step in my taking charge of myself as a thinker.

Socrates

In November 1954 I went to bed with the flu and a fairly severe glandular infection. It was an unwelcome pause in the carefree life of a work-shy undergraduate, whose activity in student party politics and in debating was proving much more attractive than reading law books. The radio in my bedroom at home had died of a broken heart. My family did not own a television, and there was not much to do other than think or read. As my fever subsided I picked a book off the shelf seemingly at random, a small blue book, printed in 1891, with a translation of the Greek philosopher Plato's *Trial and Death of Socrates*. A famous quote from Plato read: "An unexamined life is not worth living."

Socrates asked his pupil Crito: Should a marathon runner do his training with an experienced trainer or depend on the advice of everybody? The answer was implied, of course. A good trainer was essential. The runner should have an experienced coach, and if he doesn't listen to him he will suffer physical consequences.

Socrates then took his argument a stage further: When it comes to issues of morality, honorable behavior, and ethics, don't we need to have a trainer as well? Of course we do! Socrates did not actually claim to be a trainer worthy of Crito's attention (or mine for that matter), but that was strongly implied. In a major flash of insight lighting up my puzzled mind, I knew that what was missing from my life was a good life coach, someone who could guide me through the hazards and the vicissitudes of life.

For a brief while Socrates headed the list of possible trainers. People at church had spoken highly about Dr. Albert Schweitzer, but I did not really know his story, except that he had "left everything behind" and had gone out to be a doctor in the African bush where he had developed his doctrine of "Reverence for Life." I knew nothing at the time about Mahatma Gandhi's non-violent doctrine of "Truth Force." And I failed to do my homework about the Buddha, Confucius, and other notable religious teachers, and could not imagine that someone as political as my hero Winston Churchill would ever fit the bill. Father said that Churchill drank excessively. Father was a lifelong teetotaler, and I still hadn't broken very convincingly with his teaching at that time.

The Life Coach

In the end the choice largely made itself.. The choice of a life coach represented my personal situation. Jesus of Nazareth got the job of being the trainer for Peter Watson Jenkins. Only it felt as though *he* had interviewed *me* rather than the other way around. Faith in Jesus Christ was not a requirement of the appointment. That was because I made up the rules. What was involved for me was that I had to find out what it was that Jesus actually taught during his earthly life. I did not use the terms "the Jesus of History" and "the Christ of faith." That came later. But I had no doubt that it was the historical Jesus whom I had chosen as my trainer. The word "Faith" still had the Billy Graham "come up to the front" feel to it, and I didn't want to be doing that. My choice had been reasoned and was not a matter of faith. I was like a trapeze artist in a circus, swinging from side to side between faith and reason. There seemed no middle way and no net to save me if I fell.

So I devoured the gospels and tried unsuccessfully to munch on the epistles. My mother had given me a little Edwardian notebook into which I wrote sayings directly attributed to Jesus. But it was one thing to read what he said and quite another to really understand everything he meant. Some 150 years before me, Thomas Jefferson, during his second term as President of the United States of America, felt the same need. With great precision and contemporary scholarship he cut out of his Bible the sayings of Jesus, with Greek and Latin versions alongside, and created for his personal study what is now called the *Jefferson Bible*.

Jefferson, of course, persisted in his labors. I managed to lose the Edwardian notebook and thought little more about making a study of that kind until I was a divinity student in Cambridge, training for the Congregational ministry. However, the loss of the book was not the end of Jesus as my coach. His teaching about non-violence and his concern for the poor had a powerful effect on my mind. At Bristol I had been quite successful in the student Conservative Party, but abruptly, to general astonishment, I resigned my position as chairman of the group and declared that I was now a Christian pacifist. The Argyle youth group was involved in this *transmogrification.* That word means "to change the appearance of something, especially in a bizarre way," and the word just about sums up my life. I became positively interested in playing a part in the church, and so I joined the membership.

Jesus of Nazareth is a challenging teacher, as the world has found out in each generation since his time. But the New Testament picture of what he was and the detail of what he taught are a bit difficult to make out, and everybody seems to have a different take on his teaching. Jesus as Lord of Faith is much more complex. The early Christians saw the Jesus they had known quite differently from those who came later. My youthful interest was first and foremost in Jesus as a teacher. I dealt with the issues of faith with a classic denial that I would ever be able to understand them all, and so—in coming back to the faith—it felt right to simply accept what the church had to tell me. After all, who was I to pretend a deep knowledge of the Christ of Faith? You may see this as a smokescreen, but I believed that I had had sufficient training at home to realize that sorting out a coherent theology would take a lot of time and could be mulled over patiently.

The Soul

Looking back, I can't remember ever debating the concept of the soul. Although both Christian theology and mysticism have a lot to offer on the subject, it rarely came up in the churches I attended or in which I ministered. Souls were mentioned in church without fail at one time in the year: Halloween. Then the emphasis was on either the saints whose life was blessed by God, or poor ghosts who, presumably, were cursed. All Saints Day in the old Congregational tradition celebrated the saints as the departed members of the Christian church as a whole. There was no special niche for souls who had been declared "saints" by the church leaders, as there is in Roman Catholicism. This was historically because of a strong egalitarian tradition among the Puritans, from which the Congregational churches had evolved. On All Saints Day my sister, Carrol, liked remembering an irreverent cartoon that misquoted the first line of the well-known hymn, "For all the saints who from their labors rest," by the substitution of "neighbors" for "labors."

Most people of faith think that you are given a soul by God, probably at conception or possibly at death. What you actually do with your soul is a bit hard for people to pin down, and some who discussed the issue with me agreed that the soul is really what we usually call our personality. If so, I thought, some souls leave much to be desired. The problem created by people who dubbed their spiritual heroes "saints" was that identifying other people as having special souls seemed rather unfortunate: all souls were supposed to be equal in the sight of God.

Thoughts about eternal souls lead people to ask what will happen after physical death. The majority of Christians today are unsure of what they really think (or "ought" to think), and 71% of American Christians in a recent Gallup poll did claim a belief in some kind of life-after-death, the number who saw this in terms of a physical or spiritual resurrection was much smaller. The waters are muddied by talk of physical resurrection at the Last Day. So it must be, I thought, that the immortal soul carries our personality on in some fashion or other—though few want to speculate when, where, and how this strange immortality thing happens to us. Souls don't seem to be given to people as an award for merit. That issue is decided on the Last Day—the Day of Judgment—when some of us will climb upstairs with our RSVP in hand to give to St. Peter (no relation) at the pearly gates of heaven, leaving the remainder (especially those dreadful neighbors from whom we are resting) to tumble head over heels into the Pit to endure a dreadful eternity of burning and wailing and gnashing of teeth (if evil souls have any teeth left). Good old medieval stuff, freeze-dried for modern people to fall back on as needed. Dante's *Inferno* has never gone out of print and still has a message for some people. But at that point in my life I didn't buy it at all. At the end of my childhood I really wasn't at all concerned with discussing the soul. That was the gloomy stuff *really* old people of 50 or 60 talked about as they got ready to snuff it, kick the bucket, blow out the candle—whatever you want to call dying. But I was alive, with or without my soul acting like a shadow.

Polling Belief

Belief in an immortal soul has not been tested by the Gallup Poll, so far as I know. At this point in time Americans are much less certain of the influence of religion: 31% say religion is increasing its influence and 65% say it is losing influence. Also, the number of people in 2011 who saw religion being capable of answering our problems was 57%, while those saying religion is out of date is now 29% (up from 7% in 1957). There is a kind of voyeurism involved in reading the results of public polls. They come over as a sort of game, but I'm not particularly influenced by them.

In 2007 the statistics of believers were: God 86%; Heaven 81%; Angels 77%; the Devil 69%; Hell 69%; and Life after Death 67%. These figures are generally informative of the state of play in the world of faith. Back in the mid-1950s, I began to see myself bound to change direction in my beliefs over the course of my life, expecting this to happen by reason of my growing experience. In fact, I have witnessed the doctrines of the mainline Protestant churches increasingly fail to help their own people to understand and agree with their teaching. American conservative evangelical churches have been snared by their leaders' ambition to exercise political power, and quite differently, Roman Catholic churches have been throwing popular support away with both hands by their acknowledged prevalence of clerical pedophilia.

Dabbling in politics

While the un-debated soul was something to which I would return much later in life, the issue of pacifism was for immediate consumption and became a life-changing matter. Up to this point, I was politically a moderate right winger. Within a few short months of starting my studies at Bristol University in 1953, I was elected the chairman of a small but strident student group, the Bristol University Conservative and Unionist Association. My parents indulged my choice of the Tory Party, being right-wing Liberal Party adherents. They had doubtless learned by then that all the ideas of their son represented moving targets.

Before I was born, father had been a Liberal Party candidate for Parliament in the Thornbury division of Gloucestershire. He was not keen on the post-war socialist policies of the Labour Party and the aggressive unions. He read the Daily Telegraph, a conservative newspaper, and slowly embraced more and more right-of-center views as he aged. Funnily, his son drifted in the opposite direction.

Being the student Tory party leader brought with the exalted position some distinct benefits. I attended a Conservative Party gathering for university students one Christmas, and fell madly in love—for a whole four days—with a girl from Croydon called Brenda. I mingled with local Bristol party supporters at sherry parties, and was "discovered" by a managing director ("*I like my sherry very dry, don't-yah-know*") who was positively panting to hire me as a management trainee in his machine tool works. This would allow for my being able to stand as a Tory candidate for Parliament in a Labour-held constituency in South Wales. There would be no hope of my ever winning the election, but every hope of getting noticed by party bosses if I waged a spirited campaign. Were I to prove myself able, there might be an easier fight available next time in another constituency, and so ad infinitum.

The biggest prize for the student chairman was being taken to the annual Conservative Party conference by a major local Tory party supporter, the burly George McWatters, then the chairman of Harvey's of Bristol, the famed sherry importers. Mr. and Mrs. McWatters, who went together to the party conference, actually preferred gin to sherry, and had their station wagon loaded with cases of it. It was just the job for helping people to say "NATO" with exactly the right upper-crust twang.

None of these party prizes was any match for my delicate conscience, however. I had been in mild disagreement with Tory policy over the issues of comprehensive schools: I was in favor of them—most people in the party were not. There was also the issue of electoral reform. People in the party laughed at the idea of changing over our elections to proportional representation. For them, "first past the post" was the only way of running proper elections. No PR for Tories: "That's the sort of thing the *French* do." Then, to make things infinitely worse in my case, pacifism reared its troublesome head.

My ties with the Tories came to a screeching halt shortly after my reading Socrates and picking Jesus as my coach. Retaining just enough agnosticism to delay deciding if Jesus was divine—and suspecting that he was not—I concentrated on being acquainted with what the gospels recorded of his teaching about how, as citizens of the Kingdom of God, we should live our lives. Before the warmth of his social teaching, Tory dogma melted like snow. So I quit the Tories and called myself a Liberal. At the heart of my switch was the growing conviction that Jesus himself was a pacifist, and so I should become one as well.

Pacifism in practice

The first real issue that resulted from my new-found religious approach was pacifism. Discussion in the youth group of Jesus' teaching brought matters to a head. For many young people, growing up involves the rejection of ideas taught by parents, teachers, and religious institutions. Obviously, not everybody goes through this process equally, as I found out during the Sunday afternoon discussion sessions at the church youth group, which contained the usual mix of satisfied conformists and totally confused radicals.

Mr. Stanley Jones was our leader in the older group (aged 17 to 25), to which I belonged. Jean, whom I mentioned earlier, looked after the younger teens. A high school teacher, Jones was skilled in drawing out our opinions and never appeared shocked by the things we said that were critical of his professed Christian faith. On the contrary, he welcomed open discussion and frequently assigned to us the task of defending one point or another in free-form religious and social debates. I loved these mental exercises, and when he announced one Sunday afternoon that the next week we would hold a debate on a motion about pacifism, I was "volunteered" by him to read up about it and to present the pacifist case. Our intrepid leader just happened to have a couple of books on the topic, published by the Fellowship of Reconciliation, which was the main Christian pacifist organization, founded in 1914 at the outbreak of the first World War, and of which he also just happened to be a member.

I did my homework in preparation for the debate and fully bought the argument that Jesus had preached a pacifist way of life. I don't recall if my side won or lost the debate in the youth group, but I do remember that things suddenly became quite difficult at home. During the "Great War," as I mentioned earlier, my father, the wireless operator in a minesewer, had faced death daily in the Dover Patrol. Mother had lost her fiancé in the trenches. Neither of them could credit why on Earth anyone—especially their son, who had gone through World War II himself, and who had twice escaped being killed on the orders of a brutal dictator—would ever dream of becoming a pacifist. Did I really seriously mean to say it had been wrong for the freedom-loving British to oppose the Nazis? Was I nuts? And who the Dickens does Stanley Jones think he is, leading me astray like that? Father was so angry he nearly swore! (I never heard him swear.)

Battered by their argument, I nevertheless held my ground. Then I joined the Fellowship of Reconciliation (FoR), later registered as a conscientious objector, marched in protest at Britain's indefensible Suez War against Egypt, and in 1966, after my first parish ministry, took over the job of leading the FoR as their General Secretary for three years before returning to parish work. The Fellowship's Christian pacifist philosophy was all about following the loving, self-sacrificial example of Jesus of Nazareth, and seeking to influence nations against going to war, thus preserving life and happiness.

Christian pacifism should not be confused with any kind of do-nothing passivism. It is quite the contrary. Direct personal involvement in the politics of society is regarded as essential.

Pacifism is not about being meek and gentle with individuals who would rob or kill. It is a political creed that is essentially about being active within the body politic, working to establish fairness, equality, and good order among nations, with the aim to get governments to solve disputes without relying on war or the threat of war to settle the outcome.

Individual pacifists have suffered for their beliefs. In the horrific and senseless War of 1914–1918, many conscientious objectors lost their lives and others suffered lasting harm to their health as a result of being subjects of brutal medical experiments. Even today, some nations execute pacifists as traitors for their peaceful stand. So pacifists face up to the death issue, prepared to die for a belief that is intended to show others how to live. I still call myself a pacifist but have a different take on people who have volunteered to serve in the military. Unless nations make a real attempt to solve disputes before they get to the brink of war, they fail to follow the way of peace and love exemplified by Jesus.

Teacher training

Then my days as a law student were over. Most of my class, like me, either failed to do any better than scrape a degree, or failed altogether. I was very happy at the pass degree they awarded me. It was a fair assessment of a poor scholar. People said that the University of Bristol had a policy to make law degrees tough in order to establish itself as a leading law school.

The law wasn't in my future. Primed by the old adage "If you can, do: if you can't, teach!" I left home and drove to Birmingham to train at the University there as a schoolteacher. Looking for somewhere to live, I ventured to knock on the door of Chad Hill, the sole graduate hall of residence. The scholarly Warden who was technically in charge of the large house staggered out to see me, much the worse for drink. I successfully talked him down from his position that they had no room, to agree that I was a graduate, after all, even though I wasn't from overseas. So he "squeezed me" into the very large spare attic bedroom that had just fallen vacant. It proved to be a fun year.

In Birmingham, away from home and church, my spirituality became more important to me. The two major subjects I decided to teach were English language and literature, and Religious Education (RE). Unlike their cousins across the pond, who play with laws against the state bringing religion into the public arena, and especially the classroom, the British have a different approach. Parliament decided that religion—as a comparative examination of different faith traditions, and ethical standards, as well as issues that individuals face in their personal relationships, is a perfect study for children to be engaged in. In consequence, despite the overwhelming secularization of the British, RE was the sole educational subject that schools must teach, and also the sole subject from which parents have the right to withdraw their children.

Gerontius and the Oratory

While I was living at home, my mother and I enjoyed listening to the Decca gramophone, which was housed in a handsome polished oak box with a lid, and a handle that you had to wind vigorously before carefully setting the arm and newfangled fiber needle on the record. The first purchase of my pocket-money record collection was the overture to Wagner's opera *Lohengrin*. I had seen a performance of the opera at the majestic Paris Opera House, on a school trip to France. One of my last record additions, purchased shortly before leaving home, was a set of *The Dream of Gerontius*, an oratorio by the English composer Sir Edward Elgar.

The oratorio is based on a narrative poem by Cardinal John Henry Newman about a fictional character, Gerontius. The story, like Elgar's beautiful, complex, soaring music, fascinated me.

Newman had written about a pious old Christian man who dies surrounded by his friends and in the presence of his parish priest. After his physical death, Gerontius enters a place without time or space and becomes aware that his guardian angel is supporting him. He floats, with the angel's help, safely past the mouth of hell and arrives excitedly, "for one moment only," before the judgment throne of God—in a sort of Cardinal-authorized, extra-special, pre-judgment, good-boy experience. After having had this transforming moment, which is musically breathtaking, the enraptured soul of Gerontius is taken and lowered by the angel into the cleansing lake of purgatory. There the oratorio ends, and we all can go home for tea and cucumber sandwiches.

It was in the graduate hall of residence that I got to know and love this magnificent piece of music. I was enjoying the student life there, away from my parents and sister in the big house at Bath—and chasing sweet Enid, a local music student who played the cello and looked rather like the screen actress Grace Kelly. Feeling free from constraints, and knowingly in charge of my own life for the first time, I was mildly engaged with the question of my future church affiliation. Was this something that now should be questioned? Introduced by a Catholic student friend to his own house of worship, I became attracted by the ancient and solemn ritual of the pre-Vatican II Roman Catholic church. Pulled in by the sound of the wonderful Baroque music at the Birmingham Oratory - a church created by Cardinal Newman himself, - by his poetry, by the story of his life, plus Elgar's church music played on a borrowed and ancient gramophone, I was moved seriously, but only briefly, to consider becoming a Roman Catholic.

Roman Catholicism

Eagerly I applied for an instruction kit of the RC faith, which was published by the national church. They sent it to me weekly by mail in anonymous brown paper envelopes. Carefully reading and thinking over the attractively polished Catholic apologetics, however, my mind woke up and rebelled. Horrified by the reality of Roman Catholic dogmatism, I set aside all thought of ever joining the Roman church, though sometimes I popped into the Birmingham Oratory and, later, the London Oratory, for the musical treats to be enjoyed there.

Church choral music has always seemed to me to provide the very best way for people to bask in the experience of the Christian rituals. I mourn the current decline of classical music in church services. My wife, Sonia, is a professional choral singer working mainly in central Chicago churches, and I have enjoyed going to gigs with her and sharing her exquisite musical taste.

In *Gerontius*, Cardinal Newman spells out Catholic doctrine regarding death with great clarity. The good man had already received an eternal soul—it wasn't given to him when he died, as some believe. After piously dying, during which he encounters the Angel of the Agony (of Christ), he enters a timeless zone with his guardian angel, supported by the prayers of his friends and parish priest back on Earth.

These pictorial details and those that follow are very clearly drawn. But they depend on elements that I rejected both then and now: The Roman Church is portrayed as the sole institution on Earth that is divinely ordained, and without which this heavenly journey would be impossible. (Still, Newman's physics of the timelessness of the universe are impeccable; Albert Einstein would surely approve.) The whole piece is shot through with the logic of judgment, purgatory, heaven, hell, and God as the soul's eternal Judge—all combined in one vast theological treatise set in poetry, speaking of the inerrant teaching given by the Holy Roman and Apostolic Church.

This was one of the main reasons why Catholicism was not for me. Judgment is a capricious idea at best, and the church sets standards of thought and behavior that are altogether too human if not bordering on the ridiculous. We cannot have the complete angle on right and wrong here on Earth, I thought. Anyway, why should God even need to destroy souls in hell when, with a touch of the eternal finger (shades of Michelangelo's painting on the ceiling of the Sistine Chapel), the Creator of all things could easily purify, forgive, and give new life to a bunch of disagreeable, stupid, and wicked people (like me). Despite my disagreement with their theology, there is still artistry to admire in the clarity of Newman's poetry and the magnificence of Elgar's composition. That's one of the difficulties with religion: it often programs your thinking and feeling quite seductively.

Busy in Birmingham

The one-year training course for teachers at Birmingham University was full of activity and fruitful for my personal growth. Despite having scraped a pass on the Bristol law degree, I did fairly well in my studies, ending the year with a credit for practical teaching. The teachers in training were sent on visits to all levels of the local public schools, although my teaching practice was in my own choice, a high school. I filled my Saturdays and vacations by earning money as a sales assistant in the men's clothing department of Selfridges department store in the center of Birmingham. I took part in a peaceful march against the Suez war. Romantically a slow starter, I dated a couple of girls. Wow! In the Guild of Dominies (a Scottish word for school teachers), they elected me chairman. It was a meaningless student office that I was tricked into accepting, but I had the pick of the ladies for the only event the Guild held each year, a dinner dance. I wore a tux for the first time in my life and felt very grown up.

At the end of the course it felt high time to get to work earning real money by teaching. But first, National Service lasting 28 months had to be completed. I tried to escape to Kansas, USA, to study there for a year, but a fellow student, whom I admired for his debating skills, got the scholarship.

Days of Preparation

The Student Christian Movement (SCM) chaplain, Rev. Jack Newport, a member of the Fellowship of Reconciliation, steered me through the rocks of the Conscientious Objector Review Board, kicking my leg under the table when I was tempted to argue my case. His kick was well aimed, and I was permitted to give alternative service in the capacity of: a hospital orderly, porter, stoker, or stretcher-bearer; or a farm worker; or a laborer in one of Her Majesty's Forestry Commission lands. My father said he knew a farmer who was not far from Bath; Mother would very be pleased if I could live at home. Unceremoniously I turned tail, claiming that my mother's Watson ancestors came from Scotland, and it was right that I got to know the country. So I fled north to Kircudbrightshire in S.W. Scotland, where there was a vacancy in the Forestry commission's work force. There, for three months, I joined a gang shaping streams to flow better, and placing mounds of earth every four-and-a-half feet to be ready for the spring planting of a forest. Then the weather deteriorated and they laid us all off for the winter.

St. Thomas' Hospital

There were no hospital jobs in Edinburgh, but I found one in London at the historic St. Thomas' Hospital, where the rest of the two years and four months of service to the nation was done. I was mainly engaged in pushing patients' beds and wheelchairs to and from the X-ray department, situated in the hospital basement.

There was plenty of work to do at the hospital, and lots of young, attractive nurses attending the Florence Nightingale School of Nursing to eyeball. Sharing half of a scruffy flat in Kennington Road, London, with a fellow conscientious objector who worked at the hospital was fun. Roger Davies was the eldest son of Lord Darwen. He succeeded to the title on the death of his father, but he had little use for it. Our home was walking distance from the hospital. Life was spent walking and walking. It was a quarter mile from one end of the hospital to the other.

The busy X-ray department where we were stationed kept us "Conshies" active. For years, conscientious objectors had toiled in the basement, below the level of the River Thames—flowing past some six feet away—where they housed the largest hospital X-ray department in Europe. It was a heavy job with little let-up, which few self-respecting regular porters at "Tommy's" ever wanted to do. The white-coated radiographers were very happy with our efforts. We inherited a fine reputation for service. In fact the four of us were the last C.Os. there as national service was brought to an end shortly after we left.

Red-head Derek May, lanky Paddy Blenkinsop, and I often went beyond our duties, clearing late patients back to the wards (nursing units) after our shift had ended, and taking X-ray wet plates that were needed urgently across the hospital. We often helped the radiographers lift heavy patients. We did everything at the double; no, we didn't run—it was double the slow-crawl of the eternally bored professional porters. My legs and back and arms grew strong and I was rarely ill. Talk about doing a walkabout!

Pausing for a moment, I remember a strange story often repeated at St. Thomas' Hospital. The hospital had a routine practice when anyone died, either in the wards or in the operating theatre. Two porters were dispatched with the special mortuary cart, which had a concealed lower layer for the body, above which was the sanitized appearance of an empty bed. Their journey from the place of death involved using a lengthy tunnel, deep underground, which dipped down before rising again to the ground-floor mortuary. As they were trundled along, atmospheric pressures made some dead bodies expel air.

A young porter was pulling the chariot down the dip, with his older comrade at the back, pushing. As they reached the bottom of the dip, the body the newbie was pulling along let out a deep sigh. Terrified, the youth let go of the cart and ran at full speed towards his goal. When he arrived at the mortuary room, a row of dead bodies greeted him and he fainted on the ice-cold floor. No, the young man wasn't me. In fact, in my two years in hospital service, I never made the trip to the mortuary.

Evangelicals

Fortunately this book is about my spiritual wanderings and not my successes and failures in romance. I'm able merely to note that most of the nurses who weren't Roman Catholics seemed to be IVF (Inter-Varsity Fellowship) evangelicals, so I got to go to a good number of evangelistic events. I suppose that when a young man is not intending to marry very soon, he might as well be targeted for conversion. I did get sort of engaged to Tessa, one of the mildly evangelical nurses who was a joy to be with, but we were miles apart in our churchmanship and attitude to life, and eventually she beat a sensible retreat.

Evangelicals' jokes can be very corny on occasion. This one was aired at Pentecost:

> Young man: "Does the Bible tell us we can smoke?"
> Youth leader: "I don't think so. What does it say?"
> Young man: "It tells us to burst into flame!"

It was not the jokes but the mental control by the leadership of the congregation that finally turned me off their approach to the faith. My hospital duties had included working one morning a week in the small office of a psychologist, Dr. William Walters Sargant, whose practice featured electric shock therapy. My job was to keep hold of the feet of patients, who tended to kick and hurt themselves when the electrical shock was delivered. I was not happy observing the treatment. It reminded me of the tragic story of St. Francis of Assisi, who suffered a supposed "cure" for eye problems by allowing a quack doctor to apply a red hot poker to both of his eyes, which blinded him for life.

Sargant had written a book that the four of us porters devoured eagerly. It was called *Battle for the Mind: a Physiology of Conversion and Brainwashing.* On Dr. Sargant's list of brainwashing organizations were both Christian evangelical groups and such secular brainwashers as the Nazis under Hitler. The book helped me to understand my doubts about Billy Graham and the IVF churches I had visited. I recalled Rev. Coggan's "Christian Certainties" series of sermons, which had not been associated with any call for people to come up to the front of the church and give their life to Christ. Ratiocination or reasoning, à la Professor Coutts, cut the unverifiable claims of evangelical Bible churches down in size.

Warm-hearted skepticism has remained with me as a reaction in many church situations. Despite my skepticism, though, the experience of working in St. Thomas' was moving me in the direction of Christian ministry. In those early days, while I was making up my mind, I did not turn tail and run from this possible future, but the church's claim that Jesus was God, "co-equal and co-eternal with God the Father and the Holy Spirit," did not make complete sense to me. My reaction was that the formula was a human invention. The memory of evangelical churches I had attended, and of my brush with Roman Catholicism, made me wary of being trapped by statements I could not feel to be true. The more I thought about it, the further my rejection of church dogma went.

Whitfield's

While living in the heart of London and working at the hospital, I joined the membership of the Whitfield Memorial Church in Tottenham Court Road, in the heart of the West End. It is now a protestant church for American ex-pats. There was a sizeable group of young single people like myself in the church. We studied together and took part in a door-to-door mission in the neighborhood of the church, and another mission to Bow, an area in the East End of the City of London where you could still hear Cockney "spoke proper" by most of the inhabitants. One thing I did learn from the experience, which helped me subsequently in my ministry, was that intellectual people often lack people skills and make a real mess of missionary advances. Take this exchange by a colleague, a student in London for the congregational church ministry. We trudged together through a grubby housing estate, going in pairs from one apartment to the next. There was a marked disinterest on the part of the occupants. We took it in turns to introduce ourselves at the doors. I heard my colleague say in his refined English public school accent:

"Good evening, Madam, is the church relevant to your life?"
"I'll jus' arsk me 'usband."
(Calling) "Bert, is the church reverlent [sic] to your life?"
"Not today, fank you."

Initially I was attracted by the idea of persuading people to come to church and, in due course, witnessing them call Jesus their Lord. Despite reading Dr. Sargant's book on brainwashing, missionary service abroad appealed to me. Later in this story, during the last year of my ministerial studies, my wife Margaret and I asked the London Missionary Society to consider us for service abroad. We did not suit the good people of the LMS—or, rather, it was made clear that *she* had all the right qualities, but they regarded me an individualist, with far too mercurial a temperament for the task. In annoyance at being turned down, I questioned the missionary model for overseas recruitment to the church. It was far too like the Billy Graham experience, selling the gospel, counting the numbers, and yes, enjoying the feeling of power. There was also an overtone rather reminiscent of the crumbling British Empire where it was often said, "Faith follows the flag." Eventually my bad temper cooled down, and I supported good friends who went abroad as ministers.

The central issue was not the way in which the church created circles of togetherness within the local fellowships. That was fine. It was also quite all right that we should join together in common belief in God and Jesus. What was increasingly distasteful was the pressure to conform in thought, word, and deed—even in the most liberal of denominations. That was something that rankled within me.

Living in central London gave many opportunities to taste sermons preached by a variety of leading ministers. Although I had been elected to the lay diaconate of the Tottenham Court Road church, my favorite preacher was Dr. Leslie Weatherhead, a psychological counselor and the minister of the City Temple, whose sermons were little jewels. He used his considerable talents to introduce topics that were meaningful in the lives of his congregation, but presented the challenge of Jesus' life and teaching in a way that was calculated to stir the emotional response of his listeners. He had a profound impact on my thinking.

The call of ministry

I had gone to St. Thomas' Hospital with the intention of becoming a career teacher after my National Service was over, but now I discovered yet another attractive possibility. It was one that gave me some grounds for concern. I could see myself as a minister in the Congregational church. But Father was also a minister, with high personal standards of devotion, and he was certainly not going to approve of my changing course yet again. I was right. My parents were extremely annoyed by my switch, doubting my sincerity, and refused point-blank to donate money to the national church to help with my studies. I guess that by now, those following my walkabout may feel quite sympathetic to my parents' attitude. Fortunately, on the two occasions when I conducted services in their presence, they appeared reasonably accepting of my efforts. They turned up with my sister Carrol at my graduation in Cambridge as a BA in theology with honors.

My father had often repeated an ancient Methodist joke about a man wanting to become a Methodist lay preacher. Three senior laymen were listening to him. After the trial sermon they gave their verdict:

The first man shook his head, saying, "It was read."
The second man added glumly, "It was badly read."
The third man concluded, "It wasn't worth reading."

While a student in my final year at Cheshunt College, Cambridge, I was invited to conduct the morning and evening services in my home church in Bath. High up in the Argyle church's central pulpit, ten feet "above contradiction," I looked

69

over the rows of familiar faces, including those of my parents and sister. Did I make the grade in Dad's eyes? I had played a modest little trick on my father and had used two of his favorite sayings during the service. (I also borrowed two from Mr. Coggan.) When we got home for lunch I asked,

"Was it worth reading, Dad?"

"Yes, you preached very well."

That was a generous, healing thing for him to say, and it was clearly truly meant.

Looking back, it feels now that the reason I turned from teaching to ministry was not so much because I had a burning zeal for the Christian faith—though I did feel that way about the person and teaching of Jesus—but rather something quite specific and practical. Contact with hospital patients had made me feel that my faith had a lot to do with caring for people in their times of difficulty and hardship. There was a considerable amount of hardship in the hospital. I had discovered that I was good at making contact with people in distress, and felt they were helped by my concern and words from me that were intended to be kind.

Sometimes patients in a hospital are marked out by their temperament to become favorites of the hospital staff. It's simply a human reaction we have to nice people, not a deliberate act of favoritism on the part of nurses and doctors. Phil was one such human being. He was a businessman, aged about 45, married but without children. Puzzled by hard lumps under his arms, he had gone to his physician, who sent him on to St. Thomas' for further diagnosis and treatment. The doctors confirmed that he had lymph node cancer (lymphoma). Despite their use of one of the nation's first cobalt treatment units to irradiate the cancerous growth, the progress of his disease was horribly swift. Everybody loved the man. Nurses would drop by on their day off just to talk and spend time with him. He had great patience, a ready smile, gentle speech, a deep interest in other people—and we all felt that he died far too soon. I never saw so much grief expressed about a patient in any of the hospital's wards. Phil was but one example of patients who touched my heart and taught me how to live. There were many whom I remember in similar ways.

In my early twenties, I had veered between a sort of Christian agnostic reflection and being active in liberal religious orthodoxy. I had given the Roman church a chance to win my mind; several evangelical churches had held me in their pews, sitting quietly next to my current date. But I was drawn to the simplest and least dogmatic Christianity. Later on, at Cambridge, my favorite reformation leader was the founder of the Swiss reform movement, Zwingli, who was not highly regarded by my fellow students. Didn't he celebrate the Lord's Supper as an act of pledging one's life to God, rather than a partaking in the body and blood of Christ? That was fine by me. but not the churches I had surveyed and rejected.

The Day of Judgment

Christians continue to assert that rewards or punishments are meted out by God the Almighty Judge on the Day of Judgment. This was in the New Testament's teaching, yet it made no sense to me. It felt as if all the major religions based their understanding of death on ancient myth and superstition.

Hinduism sees our essence transferred immediately upon physical death into another body—human, animal, or some other living thing—in an immediate, unending physical life cycle. Islam denies the existence of any such wheel of life and proclaims that, in a single lifetime, we must establish our fitness for inclusion in the heavenly home—by following the will of Allah (God) as he was proclaimed by the blessed teacher Mohammed, and with faith in Allah supported by a record of good deeds.

71

Fundamentalist Christian groups see judgment tempered by our having held a mental belief in God closely matching the group's doctrine and having lived lives according to their prescribed pattern of good behavior. The variables are many, and nearly all of them depend on some kind of final judgment by a supreme being.

Compared with Christian evangelical churches, agnosticism and atheism depend on mental persuasion rather than incorporation in a community. Atheists point to the total lack of concrete evidence about anything that may happen after the death of the human body, rendering belief speculative. This sounds modest enough as a claim but really is not. Although their argument could help to shake up many irrational ideas held by some god-believers, atheism has an equally large problem itself, centering on the nature of proof. For atheists and for most agnostics, there is no way in which any evidence concerning death can be accepted, except for physical examination of the body. Atheists insist that because it is impossible to objectively verify intangible evidence of an afterlife, there can be no such thing as an afterlife. But this viewpoint rules in advance what is or is not admissible as evidence. There are thoughts and feelings, mystical experiences, phenomena such as automatic writing and psychic channeling, and much more that they pointedly refuse to take into account. I was never seduced by the refusal of atheists to consider such possibilities. Agnosticism was a bit more attractive, but it felt like a way out for those people who had overdosed in their youth on the brainwashing techniques of enthusiastic religious groups. The agnostic philosopher Bertrand Russell is a good example of a rebel against the typical anthropomorphic picture of God. (Read my interview of his soul in *Talking with Leaders of the Past*).

From Sedgehill to Cheshunt

National Service was at last completed and bed-pushing days were done. To finish off my teacher's probationary year, I moved my place of work from St. Thomas' Hospital to the outer London suburbs and the 2,000-student-strong Sedgehill Comprehensive School in Beckenham. As a new recruit, I suffered most of the difficulties that accompany a raw teacher's inexperience. When the year was over, I hesitatingly gave myself a passing grade, and the Department of Education agreed by giving me my teacher's license. Over the following years I enjoyed full-time and part-time teaching jobs in several schools, which made it possible for me to minister to churches that did not have enough money to meet my needs.

At this stage there was relatively little theological reasoning in the way I trod my path across the outback of human living. I was a fairly serious young man who had been working hard at the porter's job in the hospital and was engaged in thinking things out. Already, I was prepared to regard teaching as a back-up; my heart was set on going up to Cambridge to study for the ministry. Fortunately, acceptance by the theological college gave me a back door to study theology in the university. Thus I returned to the academic world, enabled to learn in greater depth what it meant to be a Christian minister.

I shook the dust of London from off my feet and, in the autumn of 1960, traveled to Cambridge for the three-year ministerial training course at Cheshunt College that would lead to ordination in the Congregational ministry. The school had been founded in Trevecca, Wales, by Selina, Countess of Huntingdon, in 1768. In the early twentieth century it moved into lovely architect-designed Cambridge buildings. I also enrolled as a university student at Fitzwilliam College for the Theological Tripos, a B.A. degree course that I completed in two busy years.

Cambridge Days

The walkabout had been serious and productive. Although I had gone in different directions—law, teacher training, National Service in the hospital, and the year's work as a probationary teacher—I had not deserted my inner spirituality. To others my road might seem torturous, but not to me. I was increasingly sure of myself and that I would be the sort of person I wanted to be.

Cambridge provided a truly happy time. My fellow students were fun to be with. The President of the College, Rev. Dr. Eric Pyle, and the Tutor, Rev. Jack Newport, were understanding people, good at making us work hard to complete the training course. I had known Jack and his wife, Bunty, in Birmingham, where the Student Christian Movement had employed him as a chaplain. Under the tutors' watchful eye, I dug deep into the history and thought of the church, the Greek of the New Testament, studies of the Old Testament, religious philosophy, and so on. I was most engaged by the Jewish prophets and by the detail of the life and teaching of Jesus. I failed to get on well with two tutors, whose tasks were to teach me Ethics and New Testament Greek.

Cambridge was a very male society in those days because there were only two colleges for women. Now the colleges have become co-ed and the numbers of the sexes are more equal. Anyway, we all worked quite hard and there was little time to enjoy social events outside Cheshunt College. I used to go round the venerable colleges to listen to the choirs sing evensong. Peterhouse was my favorite. Founded in 1284, it was the oldest college in the university, and one of the smallest. Then I discovered the delights of the university library and got a little closer to becoming scholarly—but did not completely make the grade!

Congregationalism was organized from the bottom up by the individual churches rather than by a hierarchy of leadership. There was a broad mixture of some big and intellectual congregations and a lot of small groups of people in village chapels, supported by straightforward lay presentation of the gospel. The legacy of Puritan simplicity and directness was very apparent in those congregations. We went to the villages and little towns around Cambridge to take services and to preach. I felt at ease preparing for a job where I was not going to be asked to teach doctrines I only half believed and others I accepted only out of my powerful sense of obedience to the faith of the ages.

At the time, there was a debate in the World Council of Churches about whether Christians ought to make a statement of belief in Jesus Christ as "Lord and God." I was cool with saying "Jesus is Lord." The Trinitarian basis of the formula struck me as an invention of church leaders and not a true description of the divine. My strong desire was to understand Jesus' teaching thoroughly and to become a member of the Kingdom he spoke about. I had little time for St. Paul's interpretation of the faith, and regarded the idea of the self-sacrifice of God on the cross, as Jesus the Lamb of God, in order to save mankind from sin, as being an incorrect interpretation of his purpose. It was basically illogical and did not *feel* right, making me ever nervous about Pauline theology.

It is quite normal for students of theology to go through periods of severe doubt about church doctrine and faith. Some of my fellow ordinands were equally afflicted. They mostly recovered before the final exam! My affliction ran deep. I found myself having chopped off whole limbs of the tree of belief that did not suit me. I felt relieved to know that I would be able to be true to myself in a church that was liberal enough to give room for a measure of personal interpretation. I was keen to succeed as a

75

minister, and took time to be as fully prepared for the job as possible. This rebellion was another high point in the rampant individualism that cost me quite a lot of difficulty with other people, especially those in authority, throughout my life.

Christian Ministry

When the time came for my first church ministry, I chose to go to the north of England, an area that we were told was rather neglected by the church's ministers. My little inner-suburban church at Stainbeck, Leeds, had an unadorned small building with seats for 200, but it was crammed to the doors on Sunday morning and quite nicely filled on Sunday night. When I left three years later, we had revised the membership list, taking off many names of people who had died, gone away, or lost interest, but confirmed that we had grown in those years to have more active members than we had declared before the pruning took place. Part of the church's success lay in the growth of the youth group from seven adolescents when I arrived, to over 100 by the time I left. Some of those kids are among the leaders of the church now.

The real heart of the Stainbeck success was the teamwork of the membership. Led by the women of the church, they did lots of things happily together, including preparation for the annual Christmas "Fayre." This event lasted for three days at the end of November (about the time of Thanksgiving in the USA), before the final Christmas shopping rush. People made things, saved up to buy toys off-season to donate to the Fayre, and made small weekly payments to the organizers from the beginning of January until the Fayre arrived, saving the tokens they bought to use as currency for goods at the Fair. The church folk were far from wealthy, but they were truly dedicated to its success. In addition to all this careful saving, the minister was in attendance for three days to spread good cheer and to pocket gifts of money for the church from regular supporters. This combined effort brought in a lot of money from local people who enjoyed the event and bought Christmas presents for their neighbors at discount prices also raised a large portion of the church's annual income.

My predecessor, the Rev. Constance Clark, had been their minister for over 14 years. She had retired and did her best not to get in my way. She taught me by example the very heart of her ministry. Until then I had seen parish work mainly in college terms: presenting the gospel of the Lord Jesus Christ, leading acts of worship, and doing a bit of sick visiting. Connie told me her secret, of which she was very proud. She reminded me of the ancient description of the minister as "the servant of the servants of Christ." She said,

"I visit people every day. I start at one o'clock and stay at each home for quarter of an hour, not much more. I have tea at five and go to evening meetings, but often I pop out to see another two or three families during the evening."

The members of the church told me that was perfectly true. Connie had a powerful parish approach to her ministry. She visited the members, plus their friends and relatives who were sick or bereaved. She visited people whose pet had died. She would hop into committee meetings and then hop out again to pay visits. They all loved her fiercely. They did not think she was especially good at preaching and even said I was better! My reaction was to copy her approach in the pastoral care I gave— not slavishly closely, but industriously following her lead. In one respect I was thought by the church to have excelled her record. There was a housing estate nearby. The horrible dwellings in it were made of poured concrete, and their walls ran with water when heated in the winter. There were some really rough folk living there. Crime was rampant on the estate. Connie had not visited anyone in the area for a decade or more. I made it a priority to see the church members who lived on the estate. They gave me a tremendous welcome. Many of the young people who came to the youth club were from that neighborhood as well.

The theological issues that had been so much of a problem to me at Cambridge gave little trouble in my ministry at Stainbeck. Connie had talked non-stop from the pulpit about the letters of St. Paul. I think people were tired of it because, after my spending a month of two talking about the life and teaching of Jesus, they came up to me to thank me for doing so. I was sorry that after I left the pastorate and another minister was appointed, in only three years the published membership of the church had fallen by about 40%. I learned the hard way for the first time that we are only responsible for a church while we are serving it.

Hazel

There was a special joy for me during that ministry. My wife Margaret and I had married during my last year at Cambridge, and just eleven months later she gave birth to a wonderful, chubby, hairless baby girl whom we called Hazel. She had the fallback name Mary, in case she did not like Hazel—but she is still called Hazel today. When she was born it was just beginning to be thought good to have fathers present at the birth of their children in hospital. These days many men are trained to give specific help to their wife while she is in labor. One such program, called HypnoBirthing®, uses the father (or designated birth companion) to take the mother into a relaxed state that greatly helps her through her "surges" (HypnoBirthing-speak for contractions). However, I had to go to the top of the hospital administration to ask the Matron of St. James' Hospital to allow me to be with Margaret for the baby's birth. Matron did not need persuading, was very pleasant, and told me I would be the first father ever to observe his wife give birth in her hospital. She thought it was about time they made it a common practice. I don't know whether they did, but I was a good daddy and did not faint as one skeptical nurse had predicted. Margaret had a protracted labor, made worse by serious medical difficulties. Her second child, our jolly bouncing boy Jonathan Charles, had a much easier delivery. But that time, I was away from home giving a lecture when she was hurriedly taken into the Kingston hospital in Surrey hurry, so I was unable to join in the fun and welcome the little guy..

We were happy in Leeds. I found myself in an additional, spare-time ministry together with the Rev. Geoffrey Tillotson, from a nearby church. A new fellowship, the Wigton Moor Church, had been formed in the High Ash housing estate by newly settled residents who were former members of a city-center congregation. Geoffrey and I began Sunday services in a local school at 9 am, and afterward we quickly shook hands, said our goodbyes, and raced back to our home churches. It was a fun job and, thanks to Geoff's pastoral skills, the little community grew apace. But I was with them only a few months before Margaret, Hazel, and I left Stainbeck and made our first move as a little family of three, heading to London for me to take up a new job as the General Secretary of the Fellowship of Reconciliation (FoR).

The FoR

The title of my job at the FoR, like that of the Secretary General of the United Nations, employed a corporate board meaning of the word "secretary." I might be called Executive Director in America. You may remember that the FoR had published the books that Stanley Jones lent me to read up about Christian pacifism for the Argyle church youth group's debate. I had kept in touch with the movement and wrote an article for their newsletter suggesting some reforms in the organization. This is what got me quickly noticed, interviewed, and appointed. The job covered the territory of England, Scotland, Wales, and Northern Ireland. Prior to my immediate predecessor, the position had been held by ministers, most notably by the Rev. Clifford H. MacQuire, and was recognized as a ministry by my denomination. I was attracted by the work, which involved national outreach and overseas travel in Europe. At the deepest level I was spiritually motivated by the historic statement on which membership was broadly based.

Members of the Society of Friends (Quakers) constituted the strong core of the FoR. Within the movement there were small denominational fellowships, a lively Welsh fellowship, and much smaller Scottish and Northern Ireland councils that always gave me a warm welcome. Concerned to preserve the freedom of individual conscience, members were unwilling to commit themselves or others to a creed. This was an exercise of the Quaker-led free spiritual tradition behind "The Basis," the Fellowship's quite broad Christian statement of principles:

(1) That love as revealed and interpreted in the life and death of Jesus Christ, involves more than we have yet seen, that is the only power by which evil can be overcome and the only sufficient basis of human society.

(2) That, in order to establish a world-order based on Love, it is incumbent upon those who believe in this principle to accept it fully, both for themselves and in relation to others and to take the risks involved in doing so in a world which does not yet accept it.

(3) That therefore, as Christians, we are forbidden to wage war, and that our loyalty to our country, to humanity, to the Church Universal, and to Jesus Christ our Lord and Master, calls us instead to a life-service for the enthronement of Love in personal, commercial and national life.

(4) That the Power, Wisdom and Love of God stretch far beyond the limits of our present experience, and that He is ever waiting to break forth into human life in new and larger ways.
(5) That since God manifests Himself in the world through men and women, we offer ourselves to His redemptive purpose to be used by Him in whatever way He may reveal to us.

During my three years with the Fellowship, the chief task was to join with others to help reform human society by educating people to understand that work for peace is a daily task in good times as well as in bad. We aimed to work together with those opposed to us, and help society to create a better, more just, more peaceful world. From the Fellowship I gained a precious personal gift, the strengthening of my ability to proclaim my ideas and beliefs in opposition to war. We stood for the promotion of good relationships and the restriction of negative thinking leading to unnecessary conflict, death, and destruction.

One of my tasks was, as a director of Eirene, an NGO based in Germany, to be responsible for sending volunteers to areas of tension and conflict. Another, self-appointed, task was to write news and opinion in articles and press releases. Toward the end of my time, a fellow director of the National Peace Council got together with me in publishing a broadsheet, the *Westminster Peace Commentary*. We made a good start. The paper went to all Members of Parliament and Peers active in the House of Lords. The money ran out just as we were getting noticed.

The principal work I did was to speak at Fellowship group meetings all over the British Isles about our spiritual Basis, and inform them of current political situations and the campaigns we were supporting. One of those campaigns was "The anti-chemical and biological warfare group." It had strong support from peace and left-wing organizations as a whole. They accepted my leadership and we did fairly well with our publicity. The

Fellowship, like all peace movements, was a battleground of people seeking the correct way to get their favorite message across, and to define closely what it contained. Unfortunately for me, a group of FoR members were convinced that their General Secretary was not fulfilling their mission, being far too ready to be involved in campaigns (they included Eirene) where the specific Christian *pacifist* message of the Basis was not being advanced. The Chemical and biological warfare group was their specific complaint. This point of view was the London Fellowship's issue *du jour*. I could have resisted their attack, but, tired of constant battling, we parted company at my request.

It was an exhausting job, but I took it seriously and worked very hard at making the FoR a success on my watch. We modernized the office, started a monthly newsletter, added youth workers, enjoyed increased membership and donations, and bore our witness in the dark days of the Vietnam war and the troubles in Rhodesia.

Jonathan came along while I was serving the Fellowship. We now had two lovely children as Jonathan, a bright eyed little boy, had joined our family. I was seldom home for them, and was even out on a speaking engagement somewhere in the North of England when he decided to be born. The Fellowship house we lived in was close to the river Thames, and when a tributary of that river burst its banks we found ourselves in the middle of a murky sea of river water and sewage. We knew we had to move as soon as possible for our family's sake. I had been helping the Wimbledon Congregational church, where I had been a student pastor from Cambridge one summer. They had been without a minister for some time. I slipped out of the FoR and into the Wimbledon ministry, supported by full-time teaching at the Wandsworth Boys' School because the church could not afford to pay me any salary. But they did have a very nice house in the center of the town, where we lived comfortably for the next seven-and-a-half years.

Wimbledon

It was a fun job at the Wimbledon church. We shared our building with St. Mark's, the local Church of England whose building had been burned to the ground by an arsonist. While the Anglicans were slowly rebuilding their church to a modern and tasteful design, our building was declared very unsafe. The massive Henry Willis organ had shaken the brickwork of the chancel to pieces, and demolition of the whole building was urgently needed. So we exchanged a church for a parking lot. The Church of England generously invited us to use their building for Sunday worship, and the Anglican curate and I ran the evening activities, many of which were musical and brought newcomers through our door. This was a good pastoral ministry, but because my weekdays were spent teaching at Wandsworth Boys' School, I could only go slowly round the houses visiting my flock.

I tolerated one specific activity that church sharing made hard for me to resist when leading our joint services. The Church of England members recited the creeds—and so must we lest we give offense. Not all my members were prepared to do that, but most regarded saying the creed as at least an act of friendship and at best a sign of commitment. In time, several members embraced the practice for themselves. It was not yet opportune for me to leave traditional Christianity, but I felt nails being driven into the coffin of my obedience to the faith while I was ministering at St. Mark's. In fact, our sharing experiment was quite highly regarded, being the only such voluntary sharing between the two denominations at the time. After we had moved from Wimbledon, my job was taken by one of our leading minsters, but this was when the Congregationalists in England and Wales and the

English Presbyterians merged into the United Reformed Church. (Do not confuse this with the American URC.) There was a large and lively former Presbyterian church within three minutes' walk from St. Mark's. My successor was encouraged to come with our people to join the bigger congregation. Some of them did; some stayed in St. Mark's where they felt more at home. Belief systems belong mostly to the clergy. Most people go to churches they "like" and where they feel supported, especially when they are getting close to the end of life.

Death and burial

Talking thus reminds me that people try very hard to express what they feel is the right meaning to give their experience of death. This is shown especially clearly in respect of funerals. During my Wimbledon ministry I conducted a lot of them, many more than weddings because there was a sizeable older population in my parish.

Much has been made of excess in the arrangements that are made for embalming bodies, and for unaffordable funerals that take place on both sides of the Atlantic. There seems little point in Michael Jackson's fashionable, 14-karat gold-plated coffin in the USA, and Sir Winston Churchill's lead-lined one in Britain. In the case of less affluent or less prominent people, it is extraordinary that anyone would willingly pay for a fine-quality, craftsman-built wood or stainless steel coffin, possibly also equipped with a mechanical sliding device that makes it easy for the body to be viewed high up in the coffin at the wake, then lowered gently when the time comes for closing the lid before the funeral. Doubtless, such things are sold to relatives in the state of mental paralysis that accompanies grief, who order expensive solutions on the advice of profit-minded funeral directors.

If expense is one issue in coffins, another is their purpose. Coffins are quality productions built with a craftsman's finish because there is a demand for them. Some even provide an airtight environment, in the illogical belief that the physical body of the deceased will be resurrected on the Last Day, so everything possible should be done to preserve the corpse. I heard that one widower sent his wife's cremated remains into space in a rocket, so that she could be "nearer to God."

I have tremendous sympathy for people who are mourning the loss of physical contact with a loved one. It is a precious experience to have been closely connected to another human being. Grief is generally thought to occur because someone is no longer alive, but, truthfully, it is always because the dear one is no longer around *for those left behind*. The desperate attempts we make to preserve the bodies of loved ones speak much more loudly of the fear of being left alone than they do of belief in eternal life. Relatively few people are really sure there is such a thing as eternal life awaiting us when we die—in other words, that our soul is eternal although our body dies. Religions teach little about the nature of the eternal soul, as I said earlier, and, given their teaching that on the Day of Judgment our soul may go to Hell for an eternity, it is not surprising that most people avoid dealing with such a tricky issue. I know that many older people hang on to life when there is little left of it, doing so because they are too scared by the thought of hell to allow their body to die.

Cremation was the norm in the south London suburbs when I was there, and most burials were of cremated ashes. Cremation was less expensive than burial of the body, and people in the local society talked about cremation in a positive way that helped many of the bereaved to make up their minds in its favor.

My experience of cremation was mixed. It frequently involved a double ceremony, although that practice was on the wane. First, the funeral took place with the legally mandated coffin in the local church or crematorium chapel. Then came a wait for a day or two, when the ashes were made ready in a box, urn, or paper parcel, to be used in the burial service or taken away by the relatives for a family disposal—if ever they got round to it. Many families I visited had a box or two on the mantelpiece waiting for a minister to conduct a burial in their back garden or somewhere pretty, like Wimbledon Common. As time went on, people had the undertaker arrange for the body to be cremated before having the burial service, a simpler and less traumatic procedure.

Interfaith views of death

As a school teacher, I taught that the Day of Judgment is a major idea found in different formulations in the religions of Abraham: Judaism, Christianity, and Islam. It's also in Hinduism and, more obliquely, in Buddhism. None of their views is the same.

Traditional Jews believe there will be three groups on the Day of Judgment: the righteous, the wicked, and people in between. The righteous will be given eternal life; the wicked will be sent to "everlasting abhorrence." In-between people will go initially to hell, where they will "squeal and rise again," refined as silver is refined. There are many variations for and against themes of the afterlife and judgment. In a tolerant mood, the Mishneh says people do not need to be Jewish to enjoy Heaven. The pious of all nations have a portion in the world to come.

The Torah sees that the purpose of earthly life is for us to fulfill our duties to God and man. Success brings rewards; failure, punishments. We don't need to know if rewards and punishments continue after death—or if anything at all happens after death.

Christian opinions vary in considering the Day of Judgment. Most believe that the soul is detached from the body and goes on living, but for many the resurrection of the bodies of the dead will also take place at the end of time. Many believe in a physical hell to which God, the great judge, will assign evildoers—as a place of actual physical torment. Heaven will be for those who get a pass for their belief and good works, but there's an argument about whether it is faith alone that unlocks the pearly gates.

Catholics believe souls are given an individual judgment and are sent to heaven, hell, or purification (called purgatory). Orthodox Christians place greater emphasis on divine grace: If it is true that God judges humanity mercifully, then all may receive forgiveness of their sins.

Protestants generally hold to the idea of the eternal nature of the soul and the resurrection of the dead on the last day, when they will be assigned to heaven or hell for eternity. Many liberal Protestants reject the idea of the Last Judgment, however. They see universal salvation to be the destination for people's souls. Few of them believe in physical resurrection on the Last Day.

Religions tell stories that dramatize death. Unlike the quite lurid descriptions of ancient myths, religious teaching and art have the same purpose: to assure the individual that death is truly understood, and what happens after death is known by that religion. Death provides the religions with control over the lives of their adherents. It points them to the remedies their faith prescribes to avert a negative divine judgment.

People in the middle ages first called death the "Grim Reaper," personified as a skeletal figure in a black cloak with a mysterious hood, carrying a large scythe. Common in drawings then, the figure is seen even today, when death is impersonated at Halloween. Roles ascribed to the Grim Reaper were various, from being a friendly guide to help the soul through the death experience, to being an austere, strong entity who actually facilitates a person's death. Some tales were also told of a capricious specter, or one who could be tricked or bribed into going away—for a time.

It's funny, the things you learn on your way through life. Reading Greek mythology I recall that the ancient stories about death were less grim. Their symbolic figure, Thanatos, was depicted sometimes as a fresh-faced boy, but frequently as a man with a neat beard and matching set of wings. Nice. Much more my cup of tea! To drive the fuzzy point home, Thanatos usually turned up to do his job with his brother, Hypnos, the god of sleep, in tow. (That's where we get the word "hypnotism.")

Because of the inevitability of death, Thanatos was not perceived as evil but as gentle and correct, leading souls away to Hades, the place of the dead, which was also known as the Underworld. He delivered his charge to a gaunt ferryman, who was called Charon, and whose skeletal figure was more in the style of the Grim Reaper. This ghostly person rowed a boat containing the dead across the river Styx to the land of the dead.

But what if death isn't like it's pictured at all? What if the story in *The Dream of Gerontius* is merely art, and not really truth; if most funerals have no cosmic content; if the Messiah, the Great Signs, and the Day of Judgment are complete myths? What if it means nothing that people are preserved in special boxes so their bodies will have no trouble resurrecting? What is the drama concerning death all about? The myths about death make for a fascinating study of ideas common in simpler days. I don't know how much the stories were actually believed in the past, but in the same way as people today are quite willing to read the mind of God and speculate that "God wanted" the departed, I guess plenty of people then believed in the Grim Reaper, the Angel of Death, Thanatos, and the Hindu god Shiva.

That's all right for them, I suppose. People might call these stories part of humanity's search for truth. Somehow, religious talk concerning death did nothing for me at this stage of my walkabout. Worse: some fanciful ideas become church dogma that people are told to believe.

While at the Wimbledon church, I had an interesting time working for the London Borough of Merton Community Relations Council, of which I was chairman for a year. There, local Muslims were attempting to get planning permission to build a mosque. They were met with quite a lot of opposition from the local community, supposing that the presence of such a worship center would adversely affect property prices as Muslims bought houses in the area of the mosque..

Islam is concerned with a final judgment, believing in the physical resurrection of the dead and the immortality of the human soul. Preceding the Day of Judgment will be the Great Signs: the sun rising in the west, together with the rise of the Earth Beast, then the coming of the Divinely Guided One, and the second coming of Jesus. This triggers the redemption of Islam and the defeat of its enemies. On Judgment Day the righteous will be rewarded with heaven, the wicked punished in hell. During the judgment, a person's own book of deeds will be used for the record of every deed done and every word spoken. Islam looks for the perfect justice provided by Allah, whose mercy and forgiveness will be granted to the extent that it is merited by the individual.

The Hindu community welcomed me into their homes and the gatherings of their community. They were wrestling with the difficulties between adults and their teenage children who were embracing Western ideas and behavior. Religiously, they were more open-minded than the Muslims. Hindus have a cyclic concept of the future. There are four ages, ranging from completely pure to completely impure. The Dark Age is the final stage, when social and spiritual norms are degraded, human life is shortened by violence and disease, and there is decay in nature. This is followed by the restoration by Brahma of a Golden Age.

My contact with Buddhists came in 1969 when an acquaintance in the Fellowship of Reconciliation generously enabled me to accompany an American study team to South Vietnam. The team's objective was to examine the issues of personal and religious freedom in the South, under the regime of President Nguyen Van Thieu. The team was led by Congressman John Conyers, Jr., of Michigan, who was greeted by the local people and the army as the first representative from Congress to visit the war-torn country in the six years of war. Unbelievable!

Helping from his Paris base to organize the activities of our eight-day sojourn was the Venerable Thich Nhat Hanh, the leader-in-exile of the unified Buddhist church of Vietnam. Before and after the trip we were fortunate to talk with this gentle, spiritual man, who has a world-wide reputation for his peaceful life and teaching. In and around Saigon, members of the team visited two prisons, Buddhist temples, and private homes. We had meetings with everybody from President Thieu in his palace all the way down the social ladder to the shoe-shine boys, and people locked up for political offences.

Buddhists recall that Gautama Siddartha, the Buddha, said his teachings would last for only 5,000 years. The "ten moral courses of conduct" would then be replaced by ten amoral concepts, leading to great poverty. Then the end of good world order would dominate. This time would precede the coming of the next Buddha. Buddhist teaching is that there is no soul—any idea of a permanent, abiding self is a delusion.

Religions of all kinds are powerfully motivated by the death issue. Many observers have recognized that, psychologically, there is a strong motivation for people to become adherents of this or that religion, because it has attempted to make sense of the event at the end of life that is never far from our minds—our own death. Obviously, religions are not only about the end of life. Celebrations of marriage, birth, commitment, adulthood, and the daily giving of thanks to God for the wonder of life, both human and of nature, are vitally important to adherents.

Questioning faith

As I continued on my extended spiritual walkabout to explore the boundaries of my own beliefs, I saw that most faiths are quite illogical for the primary reason that human experience itself is never truly logical. The death issue we have just reviewed is a case in point. Religions make statements that are convenient rather than correct—and most people don't particularly mind, or quietly put up with it if they don't agree. Religious leaders are the keepers of a mixture of myths, histories, metaphors, experiences, imagined experiences, and also some quite deliberate ploys to control other people. If we have grown up in a household of faith, we accepted our family's belief and practice mainly, as Edmund Hillary said about Mt. Everest, because it is there. Most religious people are willing to learn but not to question—that's far too exhausting. I was at the other end of the spectrum, appearing to myself as being almost more willing to question than to learn. But how far can anyone go with questions before the walls of their belief come tumbling down?

Breaking the Mold

Parents fear their children falling under a bus, or being abducted, raped, murdered, drowned, and all the rest, is a commonplace experience. I remember being petrified (that was quite easy—my name is Peter) when I took one-year-old Hazel to the local park in Leeds. There was a big pond only a foot (30 cms) deep. While she was happily fascinated by the water, I was silently going berserk at the thought of her falling in and drowning if I didn't save her. That was quite irrational because when playing rugby at school I learned to dive for people's legs. Yet I stayed at distance so she could experience the moment without Daddy interfering. Thankfully, Hazel did not fall in and drown. She is now a very successful hypnotist and speaker in England, with three grown children of her own to worry about.

This ingrained parental fear can be useful, however. I'm chuffed (proud) to admit that I once actually saved my son, Jonathan, from drowning. It feels a little odd to tell the story in a book full of my weaker moments, but this was an unforgettable occasion that I had totally forgotten until Jon reminded me of it.

Let the drums roll and the cameras catch that triumphant moment when Big Daddy (me!) briskly told the so-called teacher, standing helpless and immobile by the edge of the pool, to get out of the way. Afterward she said, "Sorry, but I can't swim, actually." Then Our Hero (me again) waded into the swimming bath and saved his son just as the little chap was going under for the last time. Cheers! Let's pin a medal for bravery to Daddy's bare chest. (Ouch!) Better still, help the poor old man not to forget in future. (While you're pouring, I'll have mine without ice.)

My clothes got wet from the waist down—a small price to pay in the circumstances. I'm glad not to have ever borne a grudge at the teacher (I didn't even remember the incident, for goodness' sake), and, best of all, Jon is alive, fully grown, knows how to swim, and is an IT manager, a fine photographer, budding writer, dedicated vegan, and great son.

Children's physical safety isn't the only concern that plagues parents. We left Wimbledon because Margaret was worried that our children would not gain a good education there. We spent a year in Bath, our home city. I taught on a temporary basis for two terms in a comprehensive school at Filton, north of Bristol, but jobs were in short supply, so I began to look farther afield.

Tavistock URC

My parents had by then retired to Exmouth on the south coast of England. Margaret's father had recently died. Then, because it worked out for the best financially, we ended up living in the little market town of Tavistock in Devonshire. The Tavistock United Reformed Church called me to be their minister, lending me a house to live in. They could not afford to pay me (what's new?) except for a few expenses, so I was very fortunate to be appointed to the staff of the Okehampton School, 11 miles down the road.

Following the collapse of the Tavistock church ceiling in the middle of the night, shortly after our arrival, the church members tried to find a spiritual home in any of the neighboring churches where they might be welcome to join. None of the local congregations responded positively. In the church meeting I stood almost alone in favor of rebuilding. Then I found a capital sum left over from the sale of their previous Congregational church, which had been in terrible repair and had to be demolished. The people had really given up wanting to survive as a congregation, but I was in no mind to encourage that attitude, if only because I would be out of the job I had been in for only a month or two.

The URC church got a good deal having me as their minister. By the end of my three years there, they could enjoy a long list of positive changes. The completely new ceiling, of an attractive acoustic tile, was slung lower than the previous one, kept the church warmer, and improved the acoustics. The church was repainted internally. Windows had been mended. I had personally rewired the whole building, and all the lights were new and modern. Only one church member at the beginning thought it a good idea, worthy of his time, to help me. Fortunately, he was a carpenter who had noticed rhe big job I was doing: removing and selling most of the biggest pews. This enabled us to have fewer vacant seats on Sundays, more space, and a central aisle. Formerly, only the ends of the long, boring pews across the middle of the sanctuary were occupied during services, leaving a large, empty center in the congregation for me to address.

The attractive cross I added had been cast from white metal by a fellow teacher in the school where I worked. We had glazed doors through which people in the street could see down the new central aisle to the cross above the communion table. Many commented favorably on this innovation.

It was a call for leadership and involved my slogging away with two or three others in my free time for months until— suddenly—the place was looking so "nice" that the ladies of the church got out the cleaning materials, polished the pews, bought a runner for the central aisle, and put flowers back on the communion table. They invited URC churches in the locality to come to the reopening day's morning service, and local Tavistock folk to come to the evening service. We were packed to the doors both times, and got a front-page spread in the *Tavistock Times.*

Unfortunately, their reporter picked up on a snide aside I made from the pulpit, complaining about the poor quality of education offered to older children in our town (well, didn't the prophets do the same?) and calling the big, edge-of-town comprehensive school "an educational jam factory." Following the row that broke out, a letter in the newspaper from one of many parents supporting my stand changed the metaphor from "jam" to "sausages." A few days later local school children marched into town shouting, "We are not sausages!" *Sic transit gloria mundi!*

With rising numbers of adults attending the church, and links with a new and very lively kids' drama group that rented our hall and now was nibbling at giving their support to a revised educational program on Sundays, there were many opportunities to strengthen and enlarge a church that had come back from the edge. But the 1972 union of the Congregationalists with the English Presbyterians had changed things. In my opinion the URC was becoming increasingly disciplined in its theology. The latest edict was a push to move hesitant Trinitarians like me and a good number of rural former Congregationalists, to promise faithfully to teach and preach that our church believed in a triune God, "three persons in one persona." I knew that now, finally, was the time when I had to "come out" as a Unitarian. But because of the fragility of the members' adherence—witnessed by their marked reluctance to give of their time, talent, and treasure in the way the Stainbeck Church folk had done in Leeds—I decided to take more notice of our own family situation.

My widowed mother-in-law had given up her home in Bath and had come to live with us. She had stomach cancer that was deemed inoperable, and Margaret nursed her right up to the end. When that battle was over, the pressure mounted again for us to find our children a better education than the Tavistock Comprehensive School was able to supply. So my busy three-year ministry ended, and I exchanged the lovely Okehampton School, where I had been very happy, for a tough boys' school at St. Paul's Bristol. The schools that Hazel and Jonathan now attended suited them well, but our marriage had not been going well for several years, and not long after settling in Bristol, Margaret and I divorced. She married a very nice man shortly afterward. Their time together was happy but all too short: she died at the early age of 48 of breast cancer.

The point of no return

As we got ready to leave Tavistock, I passed the point of no return in my spiritual walkabout as a traditional Christian and consciously exchanged my Trinitarian faith for the English model of Unitarianism, which holds a belief in Jesus as a divinely inspired human teacher. There were several reasons for this long-delayed departure from liberal Christianity, and I will try to remember some of them.

There was no problem with my feelings about the life and ministry of Jesus of Nazareth, who had remained my life coach ever since I made that decision as a young man. When I was not talking on personal and public issues of the day, I had preached almost exclusively about Jesus' life and teaching, and about my friends the Old Testament prophets. My theological viewpoint had settled down sometime during the Wimbledon ministry: I was resolved that, as soon as I could accept the consequences of doing so, I would move over into the tiny Unitarian denomination that was not a whole lot bigger than the FoR while I was there. My interest in the sayings of Jesus led me to create my own summary of his teaching for some of the senior schoolchildren I taught. 'The Way of Jesus" was the title I gave it, but I knew that only when I actually wrote a book about it would my desire to get everything straight in my mind be satisfied. For me, Jesus of Nazareth was a good and courageous man, a fine teacher, but not "the only begotten Son of God the Father," let alone a person "co-equal and co-eternal with the Father and the Holy Spirit" in the godhead.

At the last celebration of Communion before my departure, my parishioner and friend Mary, the seventy-something daughter of an Anglican bishop, commented approvingly on the fact that I had conducted the service as the reformer Zwingli would have liked. Embracing cowardice I told her why I was leaving, and that I would apply to transfer my ministry to the Unitarians when we got to Bristol. She promised not to tell anyone before I left.

The main reason for the change was being told by the United Reformed Church that I should teach an idea that my heart had not been willing to believe all my adult life. Another grief was the onslaught on my mind of the bigotry expressed by other people of faith. The unwillingness of local Tavistock churches to shelter my suffering flock in their pen, for example, had saddened me, though I had opposed the idea on other grounds. My memory of Billy Graham's crusade, the IVF evangelical nurses, and the dogmatic teaching of the Roman Catholics spoke the same walled-in language. Churches were power centers for their leaders, who used religion to gain status.

My Wimbledon ministry made me aware of the strictures of the Church of England when, first, we shared our church with them, and then, they shared theirs with us. Then there was the recollection of Hindu and Muslim communities cold-shouldered by the local Christian denominations. Bigotry had been very evident in the religious groups within the Community Relations Council, except for a handful of Quakers.

It was not only the nature of some of their doctrines that were proclaimed by various religious groups but also the ability of their people to believe totally in myths and metaphors, and in not a few ridiculous statements made in the name of their faith, and to pretend that, whether they were a member of the clergy or not, they were able read the mind of God.

An illustration of this last feeling is taken from later on in my walkabout. I was in an American hospital, attending a twelve-week Clinical Pastoral Education course (CPE). One sunny afternoon, a young boy of sixteen was broughtinto the hospital's emergency room dead onarrival. He had been a passenger in a convertible sports car driven by a friend. Not using a seat belt, he had fallen out of the door as the car turned a corner at speed. He had landed on his head, breaking his neck, and had died instantly. There appeared to be no marks on the body. He was fresh-faced, with the bloom of youth. When his parents arrived I sought to console them. His father sadly described him as a bit of a rebel. His mother was more religious.

"God wanted him," she said, and repeated the phrase to me several times. I learned to associate these words most closely with Roman Catholic laypeople. If anything is unpleasant or disastrous, blame God! It had been said in St. Thomas' Hospital by nurses grieving when Phil died so speedily. I heard it dozens of times in medical centers and private conversations, but it never made sense to my mind. How the hell (pardon my French) could any puny human being here on little planet Earth presume to know the working of the mind of Almighty God! Fortunately for me on this occasion, our CPE no-nonsense mentor was on my side. I was relieved to hear him say to the class,

"The boy died because his body could not sustain life."

Yes, Professor Coutts, I really had engaged in ratiocination (or, reasoning) as I came to my decision to leave the Christian church. At that stage in my life no sound alternative with which to replace the anthropomorphic God of my youth had made itself known. In a strange kind of way, when that time finally did come, I found myself not with a denial of belief but simply with a better model of the Creator—who was quite certainly *not* made in Man's image.

Religious education

One of the subjects I had taught in the Okehampton School was religious education. British schools teach children about various religions; they do not teach observance of any specific faith. When I was in my last year of teaching at Okehampton I had an interesting brush with religious fundamentalism. In one of my classes, a bunch of 12-year-olds were learning about religious beginnings. The topic for the day was animism, the Old Religion, in which it was once believed that things in nature—trees, rivers, rocks, the sun, moon, and stars—possessed divine consciousness. We talked in the class about superstitions. Several boys actually had a "lucky" rabbit's foot in their pocket (ugh!), and we reviewed beliefs in blessings and curses.

A week or so later we read in the Daily Telegraph national newspaper that a question had been asked in the House of Commons by a local Member of Parliament who wanted to know why superstition was being taught in Devon schools. My name and the school were not revealed (give praise and thank the sun and moon!). Fast forward a few days, and, as a local minister, I found myself on a local village Brains Trust, answering questions put by the villagers to the same MP and a couple of other local leaders. A man got up and asked, "Why are our children being taught witchcraft in school?" The MP, the evangelical chairman of the informal House of Commons Christian group, talked about the problem as he saw it. When I was asked to comment, I gave a brief reply about the broad-based RE syllabus. No one, including the MP, seemed to have guessed that I was the evil teacher. Three weeks later my headmaster offered me the position of head of the school's RE department, so quite clearly, he did not think I had departed from the syllabus. But by then our family was already on the move, so I turned him down—and made matters even worse for him by resigning from my teaching post the very next week.

Bristol

Returning to the Bristol/Bath area was a homecoming for all of us. My new job at St. Paul's School, Bristol, a secondary comprehensive school for boys, was situated right in the crummy heart of the city where there was a great deal of human misery and need. Margaret became the warden of a new block of apartments for the elderly and disabled. We lived in the warden's residence, a brand-new, little, red-brick house across the road, at the entrance to the St. Paul's ghetto.

The new warden, husband, and family were treated not long after their arrival to race riots. By night, cars were torched. By day, the unemployed black men of the community gathered quietly outside a little coffee bar. The local Anglican parish priest and I went, dressed in our clerical collars for quick identification, and sat on a wall with them and attempted to make conversation. They were reserved but accepted "the reverends." Then I found myself nabbed by a reporter complete with cameraman who wanted to ask me questions. Later that day, described as a local teacher, I was on TV explaining, to children watching the BBC's Blue Peter show, what all the fuss was about. Then the lengthy interview was trimmed and aired on the BBC news broadcasts for the rest of the evening. It was the largest audience in my life.

Then the Unitarians' local leader in Bristol, the Rev. Eric Wild, invited me to take pastoral charge of a nonexistent congregation at Frenchay, a village community five miles from the Bristol city center. The village was pretty, and they boasted that the famous cricketer Billy Grace used to play the game on the village green. Through the wrought iron gate you could see that the little church was truly an architectural gem. The building is a sweet historical treasure built in the last decade of the sixteenth century and populated by people with a mixture of traditions who at that time were technically in the Church of England. Later on, in the seventeenth century, dissenters were permitted by the Five Mile

Act of 1662 to establish congregations, providing they were, like the Frenchay Chapel, at least five miles from the city center.

The Chapel came to be associated with the Unitarians, and in due time a Church of England building was erected on the edge of the village green to cater for the local population. The stone chapel is now registered as a grade one historic building (the best!). It is quite small, lit by large, clear glass windows with rounded tops, and has a bell tower and a bell. The seating is for about 50 people on chairs downstairs and a few more in pews in the balcony. It possesses a neat little graveyard, with trees and flowers and ancient table-top grave stones. The only minister of note was the Rev. Joseph Priestly, known on both sides of the Atlantic as a philosopher and scientist, and the one who first isolated oxygen in 1774.

The Chapel had closed its doors some years before my arrival, following the discovery of dry rot in its wooden floor and pews. Dry rot is a galloping disease, so the floor and most of the pews had been taken away and burned. Though a new concrete floor had been laid and the remaining woodwork treated with chemicals, the previous minister was not able to finish the work of making it habitable and of rebuilding the diminutive congregation, which numbered about ten, mostly older, people who were attending Bristol's two other Unitarian churches.

The first job was to get the place into some sort of shape. I began by pulling the overgrown ivy off the perimeter wall. People stopped to talk. I recruited them to come and help. They cleaned the place up, fixed the ceiling, painted the interior, put the garden to rights, installed a new notice board a schoolmaster colleague had generously made—and when the work was winding down, some thirty people found themselves sitting with their new friends at the first service. They had me as their minister, a brand new Unitarian who had fulfilled a very simple denominational requirement of spending three weekends talking to the college president of the (then) Manchester College, Oxford, about the beliefs and practices of the Unitarian Church.

Triple whammies

This golden time was just before the first big personal disaster hit me with full force. I had mistakenly understood that the Church was going to pay me a ministerial salary from denominational funds. I had made a careless and bad mistake, all the worse by my acting upon it. I had tendered my resignation at the St. Paul's school. When the awful truth dawned that there were no funds available to pay my salary, I scrambled to get my teaching job back. The headmaster, who liked my work, said he regretted that he had already filled my post and that I would need to look elsewhere. The huge global recession in 1980 to '82 hit Britain hard at that time. The American term for that sort of disaster is a "double whammy." Nowhere in the Bristol area could I find even a three-days-a-week part-time teaching job. I was on the supply lists at several schools but received only a handful of requests. I was unemployed and had to look for work, any work. Employers said I was over-qualified, so they knew I wouldn't stay long. I tried daily to find a job but failed. Then our marriage, which had been in trouble for several years, came to an end. Margaret stayed in the warden's house with Hazel and Jonathan. I found a small flat a short walk away.

Do they make triple whammies? Don't answer; there's more to come. A new friend, Bill Billet, started a hydraulic spares depot with me 30 miles away in Warminster, a little country town in Wiltshire. My last financial reserves went into the venture. Bill was the technical expert and had been lent the hydraulic supplies. We had one very big customer and a few others. Then the big boy stopped ordering anything because of the recession, and I went bankrupt. I still was minister for the Unitarians of Frenchay. That was what kept me sane. Fortunately, after the divorce went through, the whammies stopped multiplying.

America

The Rev. Edward Frost, a American Unitarian Universalist minister, visited the Frenchay Chapel with his wife. They were on a six- month-long sabbatical leave from his pastorate in Princeton, New Jersey, and were renting a damp Somerset cottage. We became friends, and they generously invited me to visit their family home. He promised to fix up a six-week preaching tour of UU churches for me. I would be well paid by British standards, and it might be possible that I could raise money for the chapel. Delighted at this turn in my luck, I agreed, borrowed money for the air fare, and left for Princeton at the end of January 1982.

The six weeks in America went very fast. I preached in UU churches from Towson, Maryland, to Cambridge, Massachusetts; talked with the UU ministry people in Boston; and took part in two radio broadcasts. In one of these my interview was with the famous presenter Terry Gross on WHYY's "Fresh Air." We talked about the British peace movement. She was very courteous and clear thinking, but I felt that my effort probably would probably spark a conversation afterward when the station manager might say with a sigh, "Well, you win some and you lose some, Terry!"

Several times during the six weeks in America I met Julie Wilson, a member of Dr. Frost's Princeton UU church. We were strongly attracted to each other and became engaged at the end of my last week there. She flew over to Britain, and on the first of June we were joyfully married, with my children in attendance. The short civil ceremony was at the Bristol Register Office, housed at the time in a former Dominican friary, now known as Quakers Friars. We briefly went to London before Julie flew home to her astonished friends and family. I emigrated to the USA in

104

August 1982 and went to live with her and her two lively, gifted children. Julie, who was a loving wife, was a very clever technical writer specializing in computer software manuals. She earned herself a good living, and from time to time took contracts or jobs. We had a lot in common being liberal in both religion and politics.

Unitarian Universalism

In the following 13 years I had several jobs. Before being able to transfer my ministry to the Unitarian Universalists I did a PR job in New York for Guinness Harp, the brewers. Then I renovated a brownstone in Jersey City. After that came a parish ministry in New Jersey, followed by a six-month interlude as a carpet salesman because I was unsure that I wanted to remain in the ministry. There followed a brief ministry at another parish in Connecticut. Finally, because of my indiscretion I separated from Julie and resigned from the UU ministry. I found myself a new career in the Midwest, working as a stockbroker with Charles Schwab & Company in their call center near Indianapolis, Indiana.

This was a time of quiet growth in my spirituality. I was reasonably happy with the UU philosophy, although as a minister I found their openness to listen to all viewpoints was not as easy to deal with in practice as it was in theory. I fell out with an atheist group in my first parish, who considered me altogether *too Christian* for their liking. So much for openness!

The Unitarian Universalist statement of seven principles was no more binding on members than the Basis of the Fellowship of Reconciliation. The UUs affirm:

"The inherent worth and dignity of every person;
Justice, equity and compassion in human relations;
Acceptance of one another and encouragement to spiritual growth in our congregations;
A free and responsible search for truth and meaning;

The right of conscience and the use of the democratic process within our congregations and in society at large;
The goal of world community with peace, liberty, and justice for all;
Respect for the interdependent web of all existence of which we are a part."

Unitarian Universalism draws from many sources:

"Direct experience of that transcending mystery and wonder, affirmed in all cultures, which moves us to a renewal of the spirit and an openness to the forces which create and uphold life; Words and deeds of prophetic women and men which challenge us to confront powers and structures of evil with justice, compassion, and the transforming power of love; Wisdom from the world's religions which inspires us in our ethical and spiritual life; Jewish and Christian teachings which call us to respond to God's love by loving our neighbors as ourselves; Humanist teachings which counsel us to heed the guidance of reason and the results of science, and warn us against idolatries of the mind and spirit; Spiritual teachings of Earth-centered traditions which celebrate the sacred circle of life and instruct us to live in harmony with the rhythms of nature."

Unitarian Universalists' backgrounds vary considerably from church to church. People came to my parishes from a variety of religions, and from none, to find themselves a spiritual home. Apart from some churches in New England where there remained a strong Unitarian Christian tradition, I felt that it was the unitarian-Christians, like myself, who had the toughest time in many of the congregations. When people flee Protestant fundamentalism or Roman Catholicism, they usually dislike and deplore the triumphalism they have left behind, and certainly don't want to have to listen to any more stuff about Jesus in their UU church, or to be told what to think.

Some ministers deal easily with the wide diversity of people, and are creative in leading the varied Sunday meetings. I must admit having difficulty with a setup that often felt rather like an intellectual exercise and mini concert staged weekly. I had not been raised in a UU church and was never able to make the switch successfully, even though the UU's statement of their freedom to believe was attractive. At the deepest level I felt many members were rather lost. Some did take part successfully in groups aiming to build their own theology. Many felt relief that nobody was telling them how to think. Nevertheless, I was reminded of my agnosticism and the empty feeling I had experienced in not being able to identify what I actually believed. Church members gave me the feeling that they had the same problem. Religious freedom is a two-sided coin. If I remember correctly, a very high proportion of UU adherents come from non-UU churches. Perhaps the permanent student seeking a larger truth affects those raised in he denomination as well. It is hard to cater for transients and not create them in the process.

Disappointment

Life in the Schwab call center as a stockbroker was lonely. Trading at clients' request and advising them on mutual funds and the like was pleasantly challenging. I enjoyed some light friendships with other brokers there but did nothing to create a circle of friends because I was hopeful that Julie and I would reconcile and continue with our marriage. She was then living in Chicago attending the UU's Meadville Lombard seminary in Hyde Park, Chicago, with the intention of entering the UU ministry, and she invited me to share her apartment. I luckily found a job with Schwab in the Magnificent Mile. We attempted reconciliation but did not achieve it and soon afterward began divorce proceedings.

It was because of my feelings that we did not make it. Julie was generously all for continuing the psychological counseling that we had started, but I had become convinced that it would not be possible for me to fit again into her life, her beloved family, and her future ministry. It was an awful blow because I had spent the past three years hoping and pleading to return to togetherness. I had put my social life on hold so that it might be so. But some little reactions she had made, and some minor issues that cropped up when we were together, told me that Julie might believe we could reunite, but we would probably be miserable for a long time and then go our separate ways. I told her my decision which she found hard to accept. But that was the awful end of something that had been wonderful. It took me a long time to recover emotionally, and I blamed myself for pulling the plug. But I still feel it was right to do so.

The Big Bang

•

Chicago

A few months later I was working in the Schwab office when Sonia Ness came to the desk where I was sitting, covering for a colleague. She said that she was looking to open a retirement account. In the course of our conversation I told her that I was searching for affordable accommodation. She soon returned, having learned that the organist and choirmaster of the Episcopalian church at which she sang had rooms to rent. Then, having taken due note of the framed slogan on the Schwab wall: "Helping Investors Help Themselves," she quietly helped herself to me—with my happy assistance, of course.

Sonia was (and still is) a choral singer, and the church choir was one of her regular gigs. I moved into two rooms in the choirmaster's large apartment in the four-unit rectory and sang with Sonia occasionally in the church choir, as well as in another, largely Catholic, peripatetic choir.

In Oscar Wilde's comedy *The Importance of Being Earnest*, Lady Bracknell addresses the suitability of Jack's becoming her son-in-law. Discovering that he has no idea who his parents were, she retorts: "To lose one parent, Mr. Worthing, may be regarded as a misfortune: To lose both looks like carelessness." I had been so careless as to go and lose two great wives (by divorce) and fortunate indeed in finding a third, the lovely Sonia, who was willing to take me on despite my ragged matrimonial history.

Hers was less ragged, featuring only one divorce. She had one adult son, Kary.

About a year later Sonia and I were married at the Episcopal church, with a gazillion musical friends of hers in attendance. The singing was great, but so was the heat, and after the very hot reception the new husband and wife staggered upstairs, panting and totally exhausted, to the rooms in the rectory. The heat/humidity index had risen to 104º Fahrenheit during the day. Some 500 people in Chicago died of heat-related illnesses that week, including an elderly business friend of Sonia's who had attended our wedding and had a heart attack later the same night.

Sonia sang for 30 years in this Anglo-Catholic church, where the high mass is celebrated with full ritual pageantry and, as the saying goes, "bells and smells." Theologically close to Roman Catholicism, the church was nevertheless quite modern in its attitude, embracing diversity of sexual orientation as well as ethnicity. Yet, although she enjoyed the fellowship there, and was well known and liked, Sonia had held back from joining as a member. She had grown up in a Lutheran household with her father, John (who died in 1979), her strongly evangelical mother, Ann, and her brother, Earnest (Ann chose the spelling), who was 11 years her senior. He was a Lutheran pastor working in the Upper Peninsula of Michigan. While Sonia no longer actually considered herself a Lutheran, she was not ready to replace that label with another. We both knew that we would never become good little Anglicans despite our passion for the choral music.

It is a fact of life that the traditional beautiful choral music in churches is under attack. Catholics today (with a few remarkable exceptions) find it much easier to organize a pop music group for the Saturday night mass to keep the young people interested, than to hold together a classical choir for Sunday services. There are also financial obstacles: most professional or semiprofessional singers in American church choirs expect to be paid. Their equivalents in Britain usually do not, and boys and girls in choirs, backed up by older singers who have grown up in the choir, sing sweetly, often without more than medieval token pay: "Two groats for your croaks," and sometimes sing in tiny congregations.

The pattern of our life together was dictated for a time by our jobs in central Chicago. I was at Schwab until I retired at 65 and began to receive payments of about 40% of the US Social Security pension and about half of the British old-age pension. Sonia, 12 years my junior, moved from a corporate job to a nonprofit arts organization, assisting two of its directors in the fundraising department. She also sang in secular choirs with a tradition of excellent *a cappella* singing. For a while it seemed as though music would be the dominant common interest in our marriage, but one of the features of the walkabout is that, having never trodden on a pathway before, it is not possible to predict what lies over the nearest hill. I would never have foretold it would be books that would occupy most of my time in retirement.

First books

Along the way I became more serious about pursuing my interest in writing books. In 1981 I had written a little thriller about a man running away from religious terrorists. It lay fallow for 20 years until I hauled it out for revisions and, with Sonia's help, copy editing. Unbeknownst to us then, the title, *Escape to Danger*, had been used by others and was also the name of a movie, but it really seemed to fit so we kept it. It was published by a vanity press, but I made little attempt to sell and vanity publishers only work on promotion for a fee. In August of 2001 I received the supply of printed copies I had ordered. In September of 2001 New York's World Trade Center was destroyed by religious terrorists. "My" terrorists were unidentified (until a later revision made them Christian extremists), but the idea was close enough. What great timing! Now I have turned the manuscript into an ebook, and it is still selling lightly. It has had some very good reviews and one or two people say they've re-read for fun.

This literary effort inspired me to bring out my notes about the teaching of Jesus and start putting my thoughts on paper. It was an emotional return to my liberal Christian roots and my way of distancing myself from Catholic and fundamentalist theologies. I had purchased a book on the five gospels, including the early gnostic Gospel of Thomas, written by scholars of the Jesus Seminar, a liberal biblical think tank. I chose 50 of the sayings of Jesus that the scholars thought most likely to have actually been said in some form by him. The sayings made a startlingly coherent and positive set of instructions on how we may choose to live as members of the Kingdom, which I saw Jesus as meaning his ideal society. I huffed and puffed over the Greek text and included my own translation. The book, *Training for the Marathon of Life*, was peer reviewed by Dr. Perry Kea and Dr. Austin Ritterspach, colleagues in the Department of Philosophy and Religion at Indianapolis University, and kindly endorsed by the founder of the Jesus Seminar, Dr. Robert Funk. It was published in 2005 by a religious press, Wipf and Stock. Regrettably, it has not sold at all well, although good things have been said by those who have read it. One reader was so excited by its contents that he stayed up most of the night reading it from beginning to end. I have not given up on my work and intend to bring out a small popular version as an ebook in the near future.

In 1998 we decided to move out of Chicago, where we had been living in an apartment not very far from Sonia's Episcopal Church. The move was designed to take into our care Sonia's mother, Ann, who had turned 90 and was clearly in need of our support. We had to find a suitable home, so Sonia engaged a friendly real estate agent to sell her Evanston apartment, where

Ann was living, because it was too small for the three of us. The hunt was on for something affordable but a bit bigger and more accessible. It was a search that had a nasty surprise in its tail.

The red Toyota

On a dreadfully wet and windy day in August 1998, I was out and about in the family's red Toyota wagon, looking at houses in the northwestern suburbs of Chicago. For several hours I had been peering at suburban homes through the rain-spattered car windows. Finding nothing remotely to my taste that we could possibly afford, I decided to call it a day and was wending my way home in heavy traffic.

At one large intersection, the traffic lights had failed because of the storm, and all the vehicles were slowly taking turns in crossing. I found myself approaching the crossroads in a row of cars, four abreast. The car on my right moved forward and, mistakenly thinking it was now my turn to go, I did the same. But entering the wide-open road on my left, and moving surprisingly fast, was a Toyota SUV. The crash between us was inevitable, especially given the poor traction on the wet road. The SUV hit the driver's door of my car hard, and both vehicles spun ballet circles on the wet road in a Toyota *pas de deux*.

In the last 30 seconds or so before the impact, my mind went into overdrive, quietly thinking, "So this may be it," as I watched the bigger vehicle bearing down upon our little red Corolla wagon. Everything appeared to have changed into slow motion. I knew that I might die in the crash, yet at the same time disputed the idea, feeling absurdly calm and rational—not really fearful at all, although my conscious mind was also telling me that I should be. I even registered the thought that the whole experience of thinking in that way was weird but wonderful. It was living in the now and felt as if I had two brains, not one.

Then came the cars' crunching, which shook up my already weak spine so that, afterward, the medics lifted me out of the car window on a board and got me to hospital, where the doctors put me in the intensive care unit for examination. The prognosis was good (Sonia's beloved red wagon did not get off so lightly), and after a couple of days of monitoring my progress, the hospital discharged me into the tender loving care of my family physician, who promptly grossly over-prescribed pain medication for me. As a result of this error, a few nights later, sick as a dog, I passed out in the emergency room, where the doctors reported they had failed to find my pulse for a while. So they sent me back to intensive care. Although it took me several weeks to recover fully, I did so in time to help pack up our flat for the move to the very suitable ranch house that Sonia had found in the northwestern Chicago suburb of Elk Grove Village. (Yes, we have a real elk herd!)

I told my physician, who wilted at the very sight of me, that I forgave his error, conscious that we had both learned valuable lessons. But mine was not the lesson people might imagine. The twin experiences taught me that, while death is quite real and inevitable for all of us, there is no reason for us to be afraid of dying. It was not by accident that I had nearly been wiped out several times during my life. It wasn't even a warning. The car crash and the overdose were blessings in disguise. Now my conscious mind seemed to know something it had never grasped before. When the bombing experience during WWII was added to the evidence, plus my narrow escape on the Radio Flyer trolley and the incredible danger I was in climbing the school drainpipe, plus a few more awful incidents, it began to look as if either I was the recipient of a charmed life, or someone was saving me to accomplish a task of some importance. I had not really died when unconscious in the E.R. so there had been no spectacular out-of-body experience. But what had happened in those dramatic moments neatly prepared me for what was to come. When it came the new challenge came in book form, predicting the major work I would be doing for more than a decade - writing books.

Caregiving

We moved into our new home in the suburbs and Ann lived with us until her death seven years later. Ann was a Bible Christian who read her Good Book daily until her eyesight gave out. She also loved to listen to evangelical preachers on radio and television. She spent her remaining time on Earth consciously awaiting death and asking in her prayers that she might make it to 100, or even 120 years of age—the greater figure representing what one of the preachers had said was our God-given natural span of life. But she was not quite that strong physically and, despite her very best efforts, died at the ripe old age of 97 years.

Death was less a topic of discussion between Ann and me than the idea of divine judgment. She seemed to be consumed by an inner conviction that, despite her powerful attempt to be faithful to the gospel of Jesus Christ and righteousness, transparently careful to do what she felt would merit God's approval in all things, she was somehow failing to make the grade. From my perspective I saw a woman who as a child had adhered to severe moral and practical demands made by both of her strict, religious parents. She had carried that stringent ethos into her life as a wife and mother, and for the many lonely years of her widowhood. For her, there was always a right way to do everything. As I handed her the pills and supplements she took every morning, she had devised for herself a special order in which to take them and fought her failing eyesight to ensure that she knew which stupid pill ought to follow which.

From conversation with Ann, and in watching what she did to be true to her ideals, I learned how much the concept of what happens after death shapes individuals' attitudes toward dying. The fear of divine wrath drives religious folk toward strict interpretations of ancient Bible texts and church teaching. Ann wrestled constantly with evangelical teaching about the Latter Days, when at the battle of Armageddon the faithful would be "raptured up" into the Heavens. The essential consideration for being so chosen was belief in God and in his Son, Jesus Christ. But there was still that dreadful and seemingly capricious divine wrath lurking in the back of her mind. How could she be sure mental belief was really enough—if she hadn't polished the silver recently?

In the end her spirit had been ravaged by her constantly reading the Book of Revelation. Worn out by the heavy emotional struggle, she returned, with encouragement from me, to the psalms and the gospels. But her drive had gone by then, and her large-print Bible remained open on her knees every day, increasingly unread.

Ann was a tough assignment for a minister who considered himself a Universalist. The historic belief of Universalism affirms that in the fullness of time all souls will be released from the penalties of sin and will be restored to God. Belief in universal salvation was not of recent origin, being established long before the fledgling Christian Universalist community took root. In America, Universalists broke with the Calvinists (whose belief in original sin and divine judgment Ann mirrored) on the grounds that just as all people participated in Adam's sin, so through the sacrifice of Christ on the cross all would receive divine salvation.

Ann took it for granted that, it being in the holy Bible, Adam's disobedience and its careful comparison by St. Paul with the sacrifice of Jesus on the cross was wholly true. I fully understood what the scriptures said: "For as in Adam all die, so also in Christ all will be made alive" (I Cor. 15:20). My problem was that I did not believe the premise of the argument that, because of the Genesis story (which I considered a myth), the concept of original sin could be established to justify universal condemnation of humankind. Moreover, I did not accept that by reason of the death of one good man (I was quite sure Jesus was not God), such a universal condemnation would follow that could not be undone.

It crossed my mind that if such a massive screw-up could have happened in the first place, God was not really in touch with the means of undoing the act of disobedience early enough. All very well that Adam's eating of forbidden fruit could be seen as symbolic of the wayward human condition of separation from God. But that did not justify for me the necessity of God-in-Christ being sacrificed to put things right. What I did accept in all this, however, was the fact that, on Earth, negative energy being pitted against the positive energy is truly part of the nature of things.

Thinking something must be right just because it has been written in a book (this book included) is dangerous. I don't know if Ann would have been less terrified of dying had she not been a fundamentalist. Actually, I somewhat doubt it. She would have found another story, another myth, upon which she could hang her fear of death. Stories are really powerful things, and despite all the gloss and glamour, the precise theological arguments, the passionate proclamations, and the solemn rituals, at the last analysis you can say that the Christian religion, like all religions, depends on story, supposition, and myth to gather its adherents and keep them faithful to the cause.

Any debate about death must be based on more than myths and religious arguments. We must really know what the truth is and feel it in our gut, not merely find an attractive answer to silence the doubts and fears of our conscious mind. I had ended up with a 97-year-old lady who was scared stiff of dying. She was scared but I wasn't. What was going on here? Maybe people knew something I did not that made them scared. Maybe the right answer was still round the corner for all of us.

John's near-death experience

Some ten years before the car crash, I had been given a small but wholly different intimation of immortality. It was when I was taking the clinical pastoral education (CPE) ministers' course at Somerset Medical Center, NJ. The course involved us in taking turns at acting as the hospital chaplain for seven days and nights. I found myself on call all 168 hours of that week. On my last morning, the telephone awoke me from sleep at three o'clock a.m. with a nurse's request that I take communion to a dying patient.

John was a small, older man who had recently been medically revived following a major heart attack. The nurses had made him comfortable in his bed; he was awake and well able to speak to me. He quietly told me that when he had his heart attack he felt himself lift off from his body, and he saw the medical staff around him at work. Then he went into a tunnel that had a bright light at the end. When he got to the end, he met with someone he could not identify but felt was very loving, and he supposed it might be an angel. I don't remember his saying anything about the details of their conversation, but all of a sudden, he had found himself back in his body in the hospital: alive.

I had never heard of a near-death experience (NDE) before then and felt rather uncertain at the time how to deal with his story. It seemed best, however, to recognize that it was his experience, not mine, and I could affirm it as such. He seemed relieved to have been able to tell me what he had seen, and said the vision or experience had made him feel very comfortable about dying. As things transpired, his heart gave out again and he died a few days later. I never got to discuss the matter with him a second time before he left us.

The clinical pastoral education class soon got to hear my full report about John's experience, and I then discovered that NDEs are quite common. In fact, they are so common that estimates have suggested that yearly, hundreds of thousands of people worldwide experience something special at the time of being near to death. According to a Gallup poll, approximately five percent of Americans claim to have had a near-death experience. In consequence several common interest groups are monitoring the evidence. One of these organizations is called IANDS, the International Association of Near-Death Studies, which proudly claims members on every continent except Antarctica.

Near-death experiences

The modern study of NDEs started in 1944, long before my young mind was interested in or even aware of such things. In that year, the famous psychiatrist Dr. Carl Jung suffered a heart attack, followed by a near-death experience that included his having an encounter with a being of light. Jung had concluded that what had happened to him was real. His experience opened up a vigorous academic discussion, and some three decades later, Dr. Raymond Moody, a leading US psychiatrist, published *Life after Life*, a small but important book about his research, detailing the near-death experiences of 100 patients. These people had been declared clinically dead but were later resuscitated. Each study was limited to a fleeting glimpse of life outside the physical body beyond death, but taken all together the case studies amounted to a sociological breakthrough for those willing to listen. Most did not!

Dr. Moody commented about his work, comprising more than 1,000 personal contacts. Although he did not consider his findings conclusive proof, nevertheless, "It has given me great confidence that there is a life after death." This is the cautious position that has always appealed most to me. Far too many people who have read a few case studies by Dr. Moody and others have quickly concluded that they knew the perfect answer to one of life's biggest enigmas, death. But truth is not like that—it is much more complex. I am a trusting person and ascribe good motives to people who do pioneering work, but I still prefer to draw my own conclusions about the value of their findings.

In his report, Dr. Moody created a list of common experiences of someone having an NDE. He noted that people's accounts varied greatly, some having only one or two of the special feelings listed, others having most or all of them. His list included:

Hearing unusual sounds,
Feeling peaceful and pain-free,
Being outside the physical body,
Sensing traveling through a tunnel,
Moving rapidly and rising,
Seeing others: dead relatives or a spiritual being,
Experiencing a life review,
Feeling unwilling to return to their physical body.

I read Moody's first book, *Life after Life,* as a result of our discussion about NDEs in the ministry class. But at the time the issue was not on the front burner for me, and some lingering skepticism remained as well. It was not until my experence of the family's "Big Bang" that I picked up the theme again and read further in the NDE literature. One personal conclusion, based on my own experience in the car crash, is that too much is made of the hotly debated proof of death. People get bent out of shape trying to prove or disprove that the near-death aspect of the event must provide evidence of death. My belief is that you can have some of the NDE feelings even when you are not dead but in mortal danger. But of course, that would rob people of an argument.

A gift of books

It feels appropriate for me to use the expression "Big Bang" to indicate that something of great moment occurred in my life and in Sonia's life as well. In July of 2001, by which time I had retired from the brokerage company, we were blessed with a visit from a former colleague at Charles Schwab and his wife Norma. Austin Ritterspach was a leading figure in the field of archeology, and was teaching college courses in Indianapolis on the Old Testament. They brought two thought-provoking paperbacks by Dr. Brian Weiss as gifts. They had been impressed by the books themselves and thought we might also find them informative and interesting. We found them to be very much more than merely interesting. When we read them they exploded in our heads and sparked the exploration of a vast new territory of understanding. I suppose it was rather like the bombs that fell near me during the Bath blitz. Life was never going to be the same again.

In his small book *Many Lives, Many Masters*, Dr. Brian Weiss, now Chairman Emeritus of Psychiatry at Mount Sinai Medical Center in Miami, Florida, had wrestled with problems posed by an experience he had of the occult. This came as explanations and messages from spiritual masters on the Other Side, who had been channeled by a patient whom he hypnotized during her otherwise routine psychiatric therapy.

Weiss had been jolted to his scientific core by the strange encounter, which he had considered was undeniably true, yet wholly outside the reach of the scientific method as he knew it. He had an interesting tale to tell in his book, but what stayed with me

121

most was that the psychiatrist, a rational skeptic, had been convinced by an experience of the occult almost beyond his better judgment as a scientist. Although his conclusions had a lot to do with the nature of healing, he had said also that: "I believe we *do* reincarnate until we learn our lessons and graduate." What a statement, I pondered, coming from such a source.

We read two books by Dr. Weiss, and bought *Journey of Souls* by Dr. Michael Newton, a psychologist who practiced counseling and worked as a master hypnotist specializing in what is called life-between-life regression (LBL). His book detailed reports by twenty-nine clients about their soul journeys during previous lifetimes. The substance of these stories had been obtained with his use of hypnotic regression. I was much less than wholly convinced by *Journey of Souls*. The book was quite exciting, but it tried to take me further than my skepticism would allow. Now I am a little bit more accepting of Newton's work but have developed reservations about a lack of detachment in the method Newton used to elicit information from his clients.

The immediate result of reading Newton's book was to raise the question in my mind whether I could train as a hypnotist and explore past lives as well. Now that I had retired, I was free to do so. Within six months of receiving the books in 2001, I had qualified at the Leidecker Institute in Elgin, Illinois, as a certified member of the National Guild of Hypnotists, and the following year graduated as a Master Hypnotist.

Another result of the Big Bang experience was in a return to Dr. Moody's earlier exploration of NDE cases. Despite being assailed by fundamentalists on the one hand and New Agers on the other, he still held true to his conviction, summed up in a televised conversation with Dr. Jeffrey Mishlove during one session in the series *Thinking Allowed*:

"After talking with over a thousand people who have had these experiences, and having experienced many times some of the really baffling and unusual features of these experiences, it has given me great confidence that there is a life after death. As a matter of fact, I must confess to you in all honesty, I have absolutely no doubt, on the basis of what my patients have told me, that they did get a glimpse of the beyond."

Reading the stories told to Moody by those he interviewed is a complex matter. Were these people ever really dead? Some were, some were not, was the answer. The real issue was that they were, by all accounts at least, *near* death. Some of them had actually been declared by one or more doctors to be clinically dead. Skeptics latch on to the issue of death. They assume that death could not have happened completely, so therefore the story was a fake, probably created by that part of the brain we use when dreaming. I accepted the skeptics' issue, but it did not seem to me an adequate reason to reject the reports completely. People were sure that they had experienced what they recounted.

One feature of Dr. Moody's collection of personal stories was their untidiness. They did not all conform to the experiential patterns outlined earlier. This seeming disparity, I discovered, was backed up by subsequent research done by others in the same field. One person might hear a buzzing noise and feel very peaceful. Another might report peacefulness and going up a tunnel, but no buzzing. Another would stay near the ceiling of the hospital room and report seeing events in the corridor outside that the person would have no means of knowing. Another would zip up the tunnel, talk to the guide, but feel troubled, and so on.

It was important to me that those persons who had gone up the black tunnel to the light, and found themselves in the presence of a spiritual being, had a wide and inconsistent range of explanations as to who such a being might be. There was no St.

Peter with a book at the pearly gates of heaven. Yes, Jesus, God, and angels were "identified" by people, but that felt to me like guesswork rather than absolute certainty.

Again, there was a wide range of explanations given for the person's return to his or her body: "It wasn't the right time," "people needed me," "I had not completed all my tasks." No great conspiracy to defraud the poor skeptic had taken place. It was messy—all too human an experience to be cut and dried. In any case I retained a measure of trust for Moody, Weiss, and Newton. Before having their brush with the metaphysical element in life, they were kosher, scientifically trained practitioners. So were others in the NDE field: Dr. Carl Jung, the pioneer psychologist, of course; Dr. Elisabeth Kübler-Ross, a physician and hospice pioneer; Dr. Michael Sabom, cardiologist; Dr. Kenneth Ring, psychologist; Dr. Bruce Greyson, psychiatrist. I gained respect for their reports not just because their medical or psychological training made them somehow special, but because in their research they showed a commendable amount of objective reasoning.

Later, while attending IANDS chapter meetings and listening to people at the microphone relating their personal accounts of NDEs, I was struck by the immensity of this human phenomenon. *Every month* thousands and thousands of people have had a unique personal experience. Gallup reported that 13 million are living today in America with the memory of a strange, enigmatic thing that happened when they were near death. I sensed that sheer quantity really matters as a verification of these near-death experiences.

There's another side to that coin. Our culture's hostility to most claims of metaphysical experiences has the effect of driving claimants into silence. Regular people with NDEs are often very shy about telling their story, thinking it may be wrong for some social or religious reason to admit such a thing. John, my patient, had been willing to talk to a hospital chaplain; some people have tried telling their spouse; relatively few have told the world. None of us likes being ridiculed.

One aspect of the NDE experience, above all else, spoke to me of its essential truthfulness: its effect on the minds and lives of the people involved. Explaining an encounter with a spiritual being at the end of a dark tunnel might suggest an ill-recalled or even a fake religious interpretation (I think it has been that on occasion, and always remains a genuine possibility). However, subsequent changes in people's lifestyle and belief about death testify to what they really feel about the experience at the subconscious level. There has been a ton of hard evidence pointing to major alterations in people's post-NDE lives.

Dr. Ring pointed out changes of belief and personal values in people as a result of this experience. They commonly showed a heightened appreciation for life (no great surprise in that), an increased self-esteem, deeper understanding of others (getting warmer), a stronger feeling that they had a purpose in living, and a desire to increase their knowledge. Some of them developed their spirituality—not so much in terms of traditional religious observation as in the form of their inner spiritual quest. They were much more at peace as people but also more likely to be concerned with, for example, the protection of the environment.

On the other hand, a small minority had difficult or even negative NDE experiences, and not all the after-effects were beneficial. Dr. Greyson has written about changes in behavior leading to social and spiritual difficulties in the aftermath of an NDE. Nevertheless, a change resulted; that seems to be what counts most.

Peak experiences

The two peak experiences I had when in a meditative mood, have been mentioned earlier. The first one was in a conference center barn when other participants had left me all on my own, alone in the gathering darkness. The second was when I had been trying to meditate in my Indianapolis apartment, the room lit only by distant street lights.

In both cases, after the experience and a space of being silent and empty of thought, I entered into an awareness that is hard to describe except with the words that made sense at the time. There was a presence with me: the first in the barn frightening me somewhat, the second loving me gently and not overpowering me. I did not react like the boy Samuel in the temple. I felt it was an experience that could only be described as a feeling of infinity—gentle, loving, supportive infinity.

I registered an elevated sense of awareness that I now interpret as being aware of my higher self/my soul. Though both incidents were deeply meaningful to me, they were not sufficient for me to validate my belief in the overall reliability of the claims people make of having had an NDE.

It's the pattern of experiences that makes sense. The human being is composed of two elements. The first we know as our body and our ego or conscious mind. They can be observed because they are essentially related to our physicality. We call the second our unconscious (or subconscious) mind, and some call it the higher mind or soul. It is unseen and is pure thought. These two minds somehow came into a working relationship at our birth and part company when our body dies. The fact that death sometimes comes very close to us gives us a window of opportunity to view the energetic life of our eternal being for a brief moment.

When I was first jotting down the words you have just read, the memory came to me of what happened in the car crash at the crossroads. Time stood virtually still for me then, and I was totally calm, as if nothing could harm me, or even that I was not thinking with my brain but with a different, genuinely detached mind: It was a sort of mini-NDE. I was truly "near" death in the sense of there being real danger, although I was not rendered unconscious. Because of the great debate in each case about how death was actually measured, and because skeptics made a big fuss asking if the patient was really dead, I had never realized my experience was an NDE. Then, when I sat down at the computer to write this chapter, Dr. Moody's second element of common experiences came to mind: It is the feeling of total calmness. Yes! I had felt totally calm. If the SUV had hit me at five more miles per hour, I guess I would have been dead, the impact being to the door on the driver's side. Perhaps that's why I am so little affected by the thought of death these days. I've already experienced the calm that accompanies it.

Walking home

The terrain of my walkabout had greatly changed from its beginning as a child in Bath, and would certainly change some more. What had been so far a continuing appraisal of the details of my religious beliefs and my relations with faith communities, now suddenly turned sharply in a metaphysical direction. This was a situation that was much less familiar. I was no longer reacting to people's belief and philosophy; nor was it related to work I was doing. While this explosion of thought about the spiritual world was taking place I had still little idea where it would lead me. For the first time since leaving my churches I could take control of my spiritual destiny. No one was telling me that this path or that path was right for me, and this opportunity had been given to us with all the complexities and idiosyncrasies of the metaphysical materials we were studying. Now, with unfeigned eagerness, I was sharing a new situation together with Sonia who had been intrigued by the concept of reincarnation some 25 years earlier but had put it aside. It felt as if on my walkabout I had climbed a high hill. From this height the view showed me the steep paths of the hill, comprising the myths and doctrines of unreliable and controlling religions of all kinds. Now, with the new clarity of sight that these discoveries had given me, I was looking over the wholly different land, stretching out in a green and pleasant vista down there before me. I recalled John Keats's poem *On first looking into Chapman's Homer.* It might be a little threadbare, but it was a favorite of mine from boyhood:

> *Then felt I like some watcher of the skies*
> *When a new planet swims into his ken;*
> *Or, like stout Cortez, when with eagle eyes*
> *He star'd at the Pacific — and all his men*
> *Look'd at each other with a wild surmise —*
> *Silent, upon a peak in Darien.*

The Little Children

There is something very special about children's memories and their awareness of the hidden world we call the occult. Today there are highly qualified doctors and scientists involved in studying little children's reported recollections, in which they claim to have been somebody else before they were born—and often think they are still that person. The research in this field is now ably led by Dr. Bruce Greyson, editor of *The Journal of Near-Death Studies*, who is also the Director of Perceptual Studies at the University of Virginia. Under his fine direction, Dr. Jim Tucker, a professor of psychiatric medicine, is carrying on the work with children that had been pioneered by their mentor, the late Canadian psychiatrist Dr. Ian Stevenson.

Is it really necessary when writing about these topics to mention the academic qualifications of the people involved? When I first read this material I became aware that this study of young children's memories, like the NDE research, was in the hands of people who had a good understanding of the scientific method, and the study's findings were made by academics with sound training and fine reputations in medicine and science. Having an M.D. or a Ph.D. after your name does not mean you will get things right, that's for sure, but you will be answerable to your peers. It struck me, when reading Dr. Stevenson's books about children's experiences, not that the research was questionable, but that our accepted scientific theories about the nature of the human mind are incomplete, and people's assumptions must be constantly reviewed.

Innocent revelations

So, what's up with these kids? It is estimated that throughout the world, about one in every 500 little children, almost all of them between the ages of 2 and 6, talk about having lived a previous life. The child might describe his or her life like this: "When I was big I used to live in another house." He might add, "I had a motorbike," or even, "I had another mother." You might think that such bizarre comments do not seem significant in the context of children's usual fanciful talk. It is not quite so easy to dismiss. An actual example may help: a little Indian girl repeatedly made the statement that she belonged to another family and was a boy. This was accompanied by her refusal to acknowledge that she was now a girl, and by her demand that she wear boys' clothes. A claim like this, which is striking, defies regular adult evaluation.

We are talking about *very young* children, and the normal little fantasies of a child's life are not under consideration. Some older kids retain these memories, but they usually fade when the child is about seven or eight years of age.

A toddler's claim, made to his or her mother about some unusual state of affairs "before I was in your tummy," or that "I had a wife" (or husband, or children), has a different ring to it compared with regular children's babble. Add to that, on occasion, verifiable and quite accurate details of where the child says he or she had previously lived, and (especially) details of the manner of the "previous personality's" death, and the statement takes on a more serious aspect.

The first thing we must note is that these reports are made by very little children who clearly see themselves as talking about the reality of their life. Not only that, but the manner in which they describe their former condition is usually *very persistent*, and even obnoxious: like the child who claimed that his mother did not serve food of the same high quality as the mother of his previous personality had done, and so he refused to eat any of it.

In talking about the death of their previous personality, children have been amazingly precise in describing details. Some children have been taken to see the family to which they have claimed to belong. Details of the injuries that caused their former death have on occasion tallied closely with family accounts, and even with court and hospital records. Substantial evidence has been found that these children can be and have been reliable to a surprising degree. They have demonstrated unusual behavior, such as a phobia about a person who they believe did them harm. Such extreme dislike does not fit into the current situation of the family in which the child is living, yet it closely matches their description of the previous life and family.

Many of the children's descriptions have been discovered to correspond very accurately with facts in the life and death of the deceased person they have identified—this despite the fact that the two families never had any contact before the child raised the matter, and they lived at a considerable distance from each other. Fortunately, the researchers have sometimes been able to witness the initial contact being made between the families involved.

Amusingly, in some cases where the previous personality was a father or mother who died, the little child claiming to be that person has then formed an unusually close relationship with the deceased's former children—who are now much older than the little child claiming to be their parent. Recognition of family members by children has sometimes been startlingly accurate, even when deliberate deception to test the situation is played on the child. Details, such as on one occasion when money was admitted by the child to have been stolen by the previous personality, have also been verified as true.

131

In some societies where there is a philosophical or religious affinity for such issues, as in Hindu, Buddhist, and Shiite areas of the world, parents have been relatively willing to have their little ones' claims formally investigated by the late Dr. Stevenson and his assistants. This helpful willingness is not so prevalent in Western societies, where the religious norm does not readily countenance claims of reincarnation, and the intelligentsia and scientists are biased against discussion of metaphysical issues.

Social custom has skewed research away from European and American families, who have been adamantly unwilling to become involved. On the other hand, in cases elsewhere, there has at times been too great a willingness to "prove" artificially what a child has claimed to be true. These two factors have meant that out of a large number of investigated cases, only a small proportion of them have withstood rigorous scientific scrutiny made by the team from the University of Virginia.

Some small children have exhibited birthmarks and birth defects that correspond to wounds or other physical marks on the deceased previous personality that they may have remembered. Postmortem reports have confirmed these correspondences in many cases. This may be seen by some as a slam-dunk proof. For instance, following a fall, a child's previous personality, a woman, had a major operation involving trepanning to relieve swelling in her skull. A noticeable circular birthmark was observed on the child's head, broadly corresponding with the operation, and the child recalled falling onto a paved courtyard.

True to his scientific training, Dr. Ian Stevenson was never willing to ascribe absolute proof of reincarnation to any of his cases. The title of his book, *Twenty Cases Suggestive of Reincarnation* (1966), aptly sums up his conviction. He thought there was no absolute proof, even with the most carefully examined claim by a small child to have been someone else previously. Maybe there never will be. However, a lack of proof does not mean that the overall situation may not add to other evidence of a similar nature that is also hard to "prove."

The idea that NDEs and kids' stories are only *suggestive* of reincarnation does not trouble me. The scientific method requires a kind of verification—such as a double-blind test—that is simply not always in the cards. I would take as my argument the example of people falling in love. We observe others doing so and may have had the same feelings ourselves, but no one can really prove love scientifically. Not even the brainwaves of soppy, star-struck people in love can *prove* that love exists. All we possess are simply observations "suggestive" that love exists—and even those observations are probably best made in the form of poetry and song! Dealing with matters that cannot be verified scientifically, we should see that it is really science that lacks the answers.

The same is true of reincarnation. We have evidence in a massive number of near-death experiences— millions of people— and a much smaller number of well-researched, intriguing reports about innocent little children who remember having lived in the past as someone else. These constitute useful support of the case for understanding that life and death may have a different basis from that which some of us have been prepared to allow before.

We cannot say research proves that when I fired my gun and Robin lay dead with his little feet in the air, somehow he was going to become another baby robin by an automatic process of reincarnation (of the Hindu kind). Nor does it mean we know conclusively that souls in human form today are most likely to be on a return visit to planet Earth: it may well be that some choose to have only one trip. Perhaps once is more than enough for some souls.

As I puzzled out the somewhat subjective stories of NDEs, and the more objective reports that little children may know about their previous personality, I realized that what I felt inside my gut about this issue was as important to me as the process of reasoning that could be applied to the evidence. Our problem with death is diminished when (a) we see the possibility of having an living element within us that can view human life from the position of a detached observer (as with an NDE) and (b) we have some indication that we had another life before this one (as with children's memories). Actually, I feel that what is diminished is the *intensity* of death's challenge, because physical death itself does not go away but is still a universal human reality.

These days I don't see this issue as a religious one. I've been there and done that as a minister. Of course, religions work in the same field; death is a major issue explored by all faith traditions. But despite not conforming to scientific discipline, the NDE/kids' memory cases are very down to Earth. This type of phenomenon is nothing like the stories of Moses parting the waters of the Red Sea, or of Jesus appearing, transfigured, on Mount Tabor with Moses and Elijah. Nor does it discuss the reason for Jesus' death and resurrection, as Paul does in his letters. It is closer to the ordinary facts of life: as close as the SUV coming into contact with the driver's door of our little red Toyota wagon.

When you and I are puzzling out what we feel about our own death, we need to take things one at a time. I was less impressed by the content of people's near-death visions than by the profound effect the visions had on so many of them. There have been a high volume of reports from all over the world about near-death experiences. Carl Jung, the great psychologist, a leader in human thought reported having had one.

Regarding the children's claims, it was the innocence they displayed in making their assertions that meant the most to me. Those who best survived the tests of veracity by Dr. Stevenson were not put up to it by parents seeking fame and fortune. Some were blinded by such ambition but in the end their attempts failed miserably. In fact, most parents were acutely upset by all the fuss their child had caused and downplayed it.

Hypnotherapy

So this was all part of the Big Bang in my life. As I clocked into the hypnosis training course, I knew that there was more to come. The Big Bang had set me on the path to study hypnosis. I got what was needed in basic techniques from the hypnotherapy training courses. The saying that clients would teach me much more than I had learned in class was true. To be fair, my tutors, Art Leidecker and Julie Griffin (in her inciteful metaphysical training course), both predicted I would mostly learn on the job.

Naturally I wanted to experience a good past-life regression (PLR) myself, but soon discovered that just as I found taking myself into hypnosis in class had been frustrating and genuinely difficult, so in PLR it was hard to sharply visualize the variety of people my brain clearly told me I once had been—a caveman who was attacked and killed by a big brown bear, another caveman who died in a fight with a Neanderthal, a Roman slave overseer who took his life in despair by falling on his sword, a rebellious baker in the Middle Ages who was first incarcerated and later executed by his overlord, a bored French courtesan in a big chateau with lovely terraces, and a religious teacher who lived in the hills and was rarely seen by the county folk.

Those of my clients who opted for PLR were equally fairly mixed in their ability to draw information from their memory bank. Some were very good at it and had clear and rewarding impressions of their past. Some had rather hazy experiences like mine. In PLR one does not necessarily *see* pictures as much as *feel* them. It depends partly on innate abilities, and sometimes on the depth of the hypnosis.

Early on in my practice I conducted a series of fourteen PLR sessions with "Christy," a 23-year-old British woman who was living in Chicago and was willing to undertake the experiment. I wrote about our past-life work together in *Christy's Journey Through Twelve Past Lives*, which details the lives, both long and short, that she brought back to her attention in trance. The actual number of lives recalled by a client is only one factor in a successful PLR. Another client I worked with remembered more than twelve lives, but some people had a sharply detailed recall of only one or two. Christy managed to have a fair amount of both quality and quantity. She also had two early lives where historical records fitted in remarkably well with her story—a bonus in a field where even a vague confirmation of events is quite a rarity.

Unfortunately, Dr. Stevenson had little time for PLR:

> *"A marked emotional experience during the hypnotic regression provides no assurance that memories of a real previous life were recovered. The subjective experience of reliving a previous life may be impressive to the person having the experience, and yet the 'previous life' may be a fantasy, like most of our dreams."*

That is a strong statement, deserving of a reasoned response. In terms of the difficulties of PLR, all good hypnotists learn to identify the times when the client is simply imagining things. Clients themselves almost always know when they have done so, and the simple remedy is to get them into a deeper hypnosis where their ego isn't firing away strongly like that. It's largely a mechanical thing. While it's also quite true that hypnosis has a dreamlike quality at times, when they are in a dream, whatever clients say back to the hypnotist rarely makes sense. In practice, this is of very little consequence because it doesn't happen too often and is quite easy to spot.

Where I get closer to Dr. Stevenson's skeptical position is in the ability of the mind to produce metaphors. Let's say, for example, that the client is having severe money troubles. Money in some form (but not necessarily money troubles) may loom large in the story being reviewed in regression. My explanation is that the subconscious mind chooses from its database a life—at times not even from the client's own past—that has the energy the mind is seeking: in this case about money. This is one thing that is insufficiently explained to those having a PLR. Most practitioners are unaware that what people experience may not be one of their own past lives but someone else's, taken from the "collective unconscious," or if you are familiar with the Sanskrit term, borrowed from the celestial "akashic" records. I would stoutly defend PLR from Stevenson's attack that it is "a fantasy like most of our dreams," because there's a proven therapeutic element in PLR that strongly validates itself. You don't cure people with mere dreams!

During a past-life regression, the experience of dying at the end of a previous life is very common. At the point of death, or just after, the client may have an experience of the previous personality's reviewing the life that has finally come to its end. In some situations the review itself may also contain a good deal of new information about the life of the person who is remembered. Some memories in this life-review may be enjoyable, but others may present themselves with an element of genuine distress. Therapeutically this provides the hypnotist with a good opportunity to help the *present-day client* by giving soothing suggestions to ease the distress that the *previous personality* is displaying, distress that may also still be "firing" in a negative fashion in the current life of the client. This hypnotherapy can be, and in my experience frequently is, of tremendous value to present-day clients. The fact of therapeutic relief gives a strong clue to the reality and effectiveness of the past-life experience. My desire to defuse Dr. Ian Stevenson's critique is based on the proven effectiveness of the therapy in making positive change. This supports the reality of the PLR experience.

When considering the history of PLR practice, the immense number of people taking part in past-life regressions also has something to tell us. Estimates of client volume are to be found floating around in professional reports. PLR is now a worldwide phenomenon, with dozens of practitioners being trained every *month* including doctors of medicine, psychiatry, and psychology, and a wide assortment of so-called "lay" hypnotists, many of whom are also highly skilled in non-medical fields. Over the past 70 years, as regression therapies have really taken off, clients coming for PLR have numbered, at the very least, ten million people worldwide.

There is a saying: "You can fool some of the people some of the time, but you cannot fool all the people all the time." To the scientist there may be a lack of verifiable proof that people can truthfully remember their past lives and deaths. But millions of clients say otherwise. We should not forget that many of the regression therapists themselves are both scientifically trained and are highly skeptical people. They are not easily fooled into thinking that just because people *say* they died in a past life but went on living afterward in heaven or on another planet, it must be so. But even the most science-centered practitioners usually say, "What's all the fuss about?" They regard clients' reporting that their previous personalities went on living after their last physical death as just a common experience; their continuing life was as a soul.

Commonplace as PLR seems to me now, after some years of practicing it, at first I was awed by the experiences my clients had in hypnosis. Christy discovered that she had been a musician in the Middle Ages, a little French boy who died in the Black Death, a psychic leader of a small fifteenth-century English coven, a teenage Italian boy who died in a knife fight, and a mix of people from Europe, Africa, and, finally, the United States. There were clear themes in her past lives: The boys made "trouble." The women lived longer, but all suffered in different ways. Alcohol directly or indirectly contributed to the death of three previous personalities. There was one lay evangelist and one murderer among her past lives. It was a mélange that, knowing Christy a little, made tremendous sense—there was a progression in her lives that clearly helped to make her the fine, artistic person she is today.

One early PLR pioneer, Dr. Helen Wambach, a skeptic with a psychology PhD, was fascinated by hypnosis and eventually came slowly round to believing in reincarnation. It was enjoyable reading her powerful little Bantam paperback books published in 1978: *Life before Life* and *Reliving Past Lives.* In them she outlined how she had organized a series of group PLR sessions with some 1,000 subjects whose individual written reports, made after each of the regression sessions was completed, she compared and analyzed. Her insightful analysis finally convinced me of the basic reliability of the PLR experience. One item from her long list must suffice as an illustration. Although many more women than men had volunteered to take part in her regression sessions, when all the reports were tallied, it was found that the reported past lives accurately tallied with biological incidence in society—50.6 % of all the past lives reported were male and 49.4 % were female. PLR really works!

One thing that didn't figure much in my work with Christy, nor in Helen Wambach's studies, is seen as very important these days. These are the experiences that clients have in life-between-lives (LBL) regressions. When I first read Dr. Michael Newton's book I considered his LBL study to be utterly fanciful. The description of what goes on in "heaven" (as people call our spiritual Home) was so detailed it took me aback. I'm still quite uneasy with many of Newton's details, but much more skeptical of "evidence" advanced by New Age writers, such as Dolores Cannon in her books about *The Convoluted Universe*. My skepticism is still easily roused, yet there have been modest reports made by my clients about their inter-life experiences that have rung true—and I don't think I am trying to make a special case for them; other, cautious, therapists discuss the same things that their clients have also experienced.

Let me give two common examples; we have touched on the first already. Clients have often reported that upon experiencing the physical death of their previous personalities in hypnosis, they have found themselves with a spiritual mentor, usually described as "my guide," who helps them to review in detail the life they have just relived. One of the frequent comments made is utter surprise that they are now fully able to experience how *other* people, with whom they had some interaction during that life, felt about the previous personality, and how they reacted to what had been said or done.

The second LBL illustration comes from the other end of an inter-life experience. After working on future plans with their council of twelve peers, souls complete the blueprints for their new life on planet Earth by choosing their next parents from a selection presented to them for review. At this point my clients have been quite willing to describe their emotions when making their choice of future parents, and sometimes they explain their reason for choosing their actual parents. The inter-life experience isn't a blur. For these clients it is a living memory that makes sense.

Weighing the evidence

Like most aware people, I continued in my search for a personal answer to the common human question: "What happens to me when I die?" My disregard of personal risk, and my *lite* reaction to the deaths of others in my circle of family and friends, may be easily written off as denial. Certainly my relaxed attitude to physical risk supports that claim. But it may not be the whole story, because I have had a deep inner feeling that their deaths never brought those relationships to an end. This is my conviction, as I said before, in respect of Grandpa Jenkins's lovely soul.

The skeptic in me allows the thought that my strong reaction to the plight of Robin and Muffy is caused by feelings of guilt from being instrumental in their deaths. Of course, I cannot deny feeling rationally guilty about the bird and irrationally guilty about the sick cat. But, unlike human beings, these animals most likely did not possess souls, and maybe their death did draw a permanent curtain on their existence.

We examined the teaching of the major religions. No answer there. Apart from the Hindu model, reincarnation is not in the mainstream of the major religions, though most of the smaller religions do accept it, and it is said that the majority of our fellow human beings do so as well. It's also true that there was an element of reincarnation in early Christian thinking, but the church would not countenance it. Religion is of little help, except for the soul issue, but I do remember enjoying *The Dream of Gerontius* with its crystal-clear teaching that the soul survives death. It does not mention Gerontius's previous or future lives. It may be that issue was too tough for the Cardinal to express.

Then in our survey we came to the letters "NDE" and puzzled how real were the claims made yearly by hundreds of thousands, even millions of people who had an unusual experience that happened when they were near to death, or even were clinically assessed to have died. Their experiences certainly varied in content but left an indelible mark on their hearts and minds. Frequently observers witnessed them changing their lives in positive ways, and having a reaction that rendered them content to face death again without fear. It is, of course, easy to pick apart single instances of the NDE, but it's hard to pretend the numbers don't mean anything. The study of near-death experiences has moved from mere theory to something much more cogent: lots and lots of people sharing the same or similar experiences.

Next the children come, with little piping voices, insistently telling their disbelieving parents they are really someone else. If it were not for the high standing of Dr. Stevenson among his peers, one might be tempted to discount the 40 years of his work and the thousands of reports he authored. The evidence is there and, while for him it may be only "suggestive" of reincarnation, it is very powerfully presented.

Finally, we viewed hypnotic regression for both past-life and between-life experiences. Here, demands for *proof* are rather harder to satisfy, except for two highly persuasive elements: (1) the huge volume of those who have received PLR and LBL regression—a factor that must be borne in mind in assessing whether it really is effective; (2) the quality and expertise of practitioners who will tell you, from working with believers and skeptics alike, that positive reports are commonplace: the essence of souls who have been incarnate in human beings does move from human life, through death, into a continuing life beyond planet Earth. This transition happens many times in each individual's existence as a spiritual entity. We are on a veritable wheel of life, though one in which we make decisions of what we want to do and where we want to go to undertake a new life.

What comes finally in the spiritual walkabout is sure to stretch your credulity once again. It seems fair to church people and folk outside the churches, temples, and mosques, to demand of those who work in this spiritual field should not pretend spiritual knowledge that they claim is reliable when it is not. Compared with first century Gnosticism I suppose New Age writings are much on a par, which in my book is unbelievable!

As you have read, I moved away from the religion of my youth and did not buy the ordered statements of evangelicalism and Roman Catholicism, based on the biblical logic and dogmatism. But they did try to sound convincing and well grounded. New Age writings, however, thrive by calling on people's imagination. That is not a complete waste of time presumably, but speakers and writers often manage to talk about things they haven't seen, and give others advice with no basis in a well-grounded philosophy.

Now I've well and truly shot my bolt with those remarks. I will ask you to examine a setup that many people tell us they believe is pretended and false. Here' hoping that in my feeble last days I can still present to you an adequate and attractive account of what I found at the end of my spiritual walkabout, that has fulfilled my hopes and given me a great deal of joyful satisfaction.

The Ascended Masters

On a fine, crisp October weekend in 2003, I was at the annual Mid-America Hypnosis Conference, minding a table designed to interest people in buying hypnosis recordings I had created. People straggled in and out from the lectures and seminars that went on all day in various rooms of the hotel in Skokie, north of Chicago. Business was light that afternoon. There were hardly any stall holders in the room, let alone anyone with a nose for fabulous hypnosis CDs at bargain prices that are doomed to sell badly, even at a hypnosis conference.

Toni Winninger and I had met briefly before. Sonia had taken a hypnosis training class together with her and had told me that Toni had been a criminal prosecutor in the Chicago area before her fairly recent retirement. Now she was a psychic channeler or something. I didn't know anything about that sort of thing, but needing conversation to stave off boredom I sauntered over to her table where a card said she was offering "Readings"—whatever they might be. Yes, I really didn't really know what that entailed, except that psychics in seaside towns offered them for holidaymakers to buy.

"What's all this stuff about channeling?" I asked her a little aggressively. I was nobody's fool. She gave me a mild answer, had me sit down, and told me the story of how one day she had begun to receive messages in her head. They did not come to her as a voice, more a silent vibration that she instinctively knew how to

145

translate. The messages she had been receiving informed her that the vibrations were coming from a group of spirit guides on the Other Side who wanted to use her as their channel. She had complete freedom of choice, however, and could say "no" to them if she wanted, and they would go away if that was her decision.

Well, of course, Toni had said "yes," and by that time, the group of spiritual teachers who called themselves "Ascended Masters" had been chatting with her for several weeks. She had discovered that it was possible to channel answers to other people's questions, but that it wasn't at all easy to do on the spot. She knew that she needed more practice. At that time, when we first met, she was listening through headphones to clients asking their questions, a scarf over her closed eyes against distractions, as she tried to concentrate on the vibrational answers in her head.

This was all very intriguing to someone like me who had been raised with the Bible stories of Samuel, with the voice calling him three times; of the prophet Elijah who heard "a still small voice" after the massive storm; and Saul of Tarsus, renamed Paul after hearing the voice of Jesus on the Damascus road. In addition to biblical stories were tales of people who had had visions or heard voices—like Saint Joan of Arc and Bernadette Soubirous of Lourdes. So it wasn't too great a stretch of my credulity to go along a little way at first with what Toni was telling me.

With both of us ignoring the price tag for her readings, I asked a question or two about my family on the other side of the Atlantic, and the Masters gave me clear and helpful answers, saying how each of my loved ones was doing. It didn't *feel* like that unbelievable New Age stuff that I had decided did not inspire me and with which I was very reluctant to be involved. I could not evaluate exactly what was happening in this cosmic interchange involving little me and the large group of Masters, but knew instinctively it was quite benign at worst, and totally amazing at best. My first feeling was right; it is amazing!

Being now semi-retired I had flexible time, so before finishing our conversation we agreed that I would provide support for a few weeks and help Toni to refine her channeling technique. Soon we began meeting on Wednesdays at her office in the local Spiritual Awakening Center in Des Plaines, Illinois, of which she was then co-director. We still meet weekly, Only these days she drives to my home with her little dog Barkley, and we order out from Peapod, the local Chinese restaurant, when our work session is done. Their egg rolls are out of this world!

The development of our relationship with the Ascended Masters (as they called themselves initially) followed a steady course. Toni became much more at ease when channeling their answers to my questions. She soon stopped using headphones, was open eyed when translating their messages, and shed a few minor mannerisms she had adopted at the beginning. Nowadays she switches on the Masters so directly that it's quite hard to know in group sessions when she is or is not talking on their behalf. Also, while she automatically translates the vibrations they send her, she has no idea of what she has said until after she has heard herself speaking the words in English. She is a clear channel, a fairly rare breed among her peers, and does not need to be in a full hypnotic trance to do her work. She advises a lot of private clients who frequently come back for more. I think she is about as good as you get. (Actually, I think she's the best!)

Working with master spirits

In the years that have passed since that first meeting, like Jonah, swallowed by a whale, I have become wholly involved in making the Masters' teaching better known, and relinquishing my former skepticism of their work. Mind you, channeling does have its fair share of problems: Some people pretend to do it, others do it with the wrong contacts on the Other Side. But in the decade spent working closely with Toni's Ascended Masters, I have become convinced of their incredible worth. I trust them to deliver the truth as they know it, within the limits of such conversations. One big limitation is that they normally answer only in regard of what is happening in the present moment. Thus they can tell you quite clearly what people are currently thinking or doing, but are unable to second guess what they might do in the future, given the law that all souls have freedom to choose their own path.

In our weekly sessions, Toni and I quickly graduated from talking about my family and friends, and current world events, to discussing meatier issues of life and death. We raised health issues, hypnotism, Reiki, conventional and alternative medicine. I plucked up my courage and asked to speak to the soul of my former wife, Margaret. They quickly arranged that, and I was able to tell her how sorry I felt for being such a dreadful husband. She sweetly replied, saying that she could have tried harder as well, which felt very loving and forgiving. This conversation had me feeling understandably nervous at the outset, but I did not doubt that I had spoken to her. The energy felt right.

The conversation with Margaret and the positive results from our chats with the Masters about health and healing (some of which we had tape-recorded), gave me the bright idea of interviewing the souls of people of importance in society who had died. Death hadn't stopped me from having my interchange with Margaret, so why not also talk with someone like... like... Carl Jung for example? His name may have occurred to me because I knew he had reported having a near-death experience. That's just a guess, I now know without a doubt that the Masters often communicate ideas that I innocently consider my own.

Interviewing Carl Jung was readily agreed with our spirit guides, the Masters, and with the soul of Dr. Jung itself. We say "itself" concerning a soul because it has no gender in its energetic state. The interview went off very much as planned: I read pre-arranged questions resulting from my research on the Internet, and we had a few friendly unscripted exchanges as well. Toni channeled the replies given her by Jung, and we recorded the interview for subsequent transcription.

When it came to transcribing what had been said, we discovered several little inaccuracies and grammatical mistakes on the tape needing to be cleared up for a finished manuscript. Sonia helped the process by copy editing the transcript. She has a well-developed understanding of American English, and our aim was to have the manuscript finished to the high standard of *The Chicago Manual of Style*. Once these changes had been made, Toni read it over to Jung's soul, who was able to make corrections and add further to its replies. This editing procedure became the standard practice we use in preparing all our publications.

Encouraged by this success we decided to write first one book, and then a matching pair of soul interview books. I created a total of 57 research portfolios, aimed at discovering enough material about people from the past to design meaningful interviews. There were never any illusions in our minds that these were anything like expert analyses of the lives of those souls we were privileged to interview. To date, we have received no indication from readers that we did a poor job. Most readers have said how much they did not know about our subjects.

We ended up having created a trilogy of books: *Talking with Leaders of the Past* (15 interviews), *Talking with Twentieth-Century Women* (21), and *Talking with Twentieth-Century Men* (21). My prior human contact with those interviewed had been very slight: I had once been in a Bristol University audience addressed by Winston Churchill, and I had spoken briefly to

Bertrand Russell at a peace rally in Trafalgar Square, London, where we both had addressed the crowd. Having failed in a year and a half search to interest an agent or a publisher in the books, Toni and I took the reins in our hands. We incorporated a company, Celestial Voices, Inc., and published them ourselves.

There was a mad scramble on my part to "bull up" on the famous people we had selected for interview ("bulling up" British army boots to make them shine is done with spit and polish). But in my preparations I noted a large number of issues and historical incidents that were totally new to me. For example, I had never studied Jung's work and knew nothing at all about his concept of Synchronicity. Nor had I followed the history of Charles Darwin's career as it evolved. I had no knowledge at all of Golda Meir, Wilma Rudolph, or Ella Fitzgerald who were picked out from other people's lists of people who were public figures during their lifetimes.

Toni expressed similar feelings; in fact, she kindly said that she knew rather less about many characters than I did. Yet the interviews that we recorded—with my asking and commenting on the basis of my research, and Toni's answering with whatever was transmitted in vibrational language to her head from each soul concerned—was smooth-flowing and full of meaty content. I was aware that different souls spoke quite uniquely, using different words and English constructions. And there were many surprises.

Carl Jung was the first soul to admit that he had changed his opinion about something since returning Home on the Other Side. This was his former concept of Synchronicity, which he now regards as inaccurate. Then Pope John XXIII had some fierce things to say about current Roman Catholic teaching and practice. Charles Darwin had clearly softened his stance on evolution. The two-part interview with Hitler was mind-blowing as the Führer's soul described basic agreements among souls that had preceded its incarnation. Florence Nightingale gave me a verbal slap in the face for asking an indelicate question about her relationship with Sidney Herbert. Winston Churchill groused that some historians had treated him badly. Barbara Jordan admitted to having previously been incarnate as the philosopher Plato. Amelia Earhart told me that I could not contact her navigator, Fred Noonan: he was no longer available—having reincarnated and was in a career as an electronics engineer.

These are only a few illustrations of the idiosyncrasies that defied any pretense on the part of Toni, who often expressed surprise herself at such details when the interview was finished. It all was helpfully messy, however, because that made it feel right. The souls of the dead go on living and evolving as souls. Time does not exist for them where they are now, but there is progression in their living and thinking. They all seemed to have their finger on the pulse of the world. Georgia O'Keeffe continues to visit "her" hacienda and favorite mountain in New Mexico; George Orwell, Margaret Sanger, and Rachel Carson keep abreast of our planet's environmental issues; Judy Garland had a lot to say about recent Hollywood movies. Albert Einstein made it clear that he is a strong supporter of our work. He was deeply involved in monitoring the world's march toward major global change.

If any of those lovely souls whom I interviewed would understand the nature of death, I suppose it might be Sylvia Plath, Judy Garland, Ernest Hemingway, and Adolf Hitler, all of whom had committed suicide in their recent past life. Amelia Earhart had knowingly accepted a potentially fatal risk; Anne Frank, Sharon Tate, Mahatma Gandhi, Dr. Martin Luther King Jr., Selena Quintanilla-Perez, and Marilyn Monroe had all been murdered. None of them made a big deal out of it. After all, their souls were still alive and were talking with me. They told me in various ways, with the Masters filling in some of the details, aspects of the nature of physical death from their perspective.

Gone from the vocabulary of spirits on the other side is the concept of physical resurrection. Not that it is impossible—everything is possible in the energetic universe—but the physical body is a tool; they call it our "shell," as if we were some kind of tortoise. It is a necessary part of our being human. Planet Earth has been engineered to be the most tactile of all the planets used by souls. It is a place of sharp contrasts—lovely sunsets and terrifying earthquakes; refined living and squalid surviving. Planet Earth is a duality, equally polarized, both physically and spiritually, between positive and negative forces, and between the basic opposed emotions of love and of fear that lie at the root of all human psychological response.

Journey of the soul

Into Earth's polarized situation come souls who are energetic, as opposed to physical, by nature. Unlike some other planets that they may choose to visit in their regular amorphous (cloudlike) form, planet Earth requires that they become wholly physical in their nature as well as retaining non-physical energy at their core. Everything about the physical universe, as Einstein proved over 100 years ago to the satisfaction of physical science, is energetic. There are variations: the energy core of a soul incarnate in a human body is of a very much higher dimensional wavelength than the body/shell it inhabits. That remains true at all times during its incarnation.

The soul incarnates by pouring into the baby body/shell the portion of its nonphysical energy that it has chosen to bring down to Earth. Effectively, the soul has limited itself to being confined within heavy energy from the moment of incarnation until the moment of the human's physical death. Just as it takes very little time to engage the body/shell, so also is the soul able to disengage and depart from its shell instantaneously. It is useful to envision the process as being quite similar to a near-death experience. In an NDE, a thinking element of the person escapes from the physical trauma of its body. It may stop on the ceiling of the hospital, hover above the body, or travel beyond planet Earth altogether through a dark tunnel into a realm of light. It's a process the soul follows without difficulty.

The energy of the soul is of a different, non-tactile nature when compared with that of the physical body. The purpose of the soul's chosen exercise requires that the spiritual element is expressed at all times through the physical body. So it is that, although no physical body is able to sustain itself without the supportive, life-giving presence of the soul, neither is the energy of the soul without restrictions. The ego-centered body/shell is able to temporarily overpower the softly made requests of the "higher mind." In some cases where our soul is overwhelmed by our human ego it will render the individual soul's incarnation a virtual waste of time in terms of the chosen lessons that it may have failed to learn. We don't arrive on Earth and have it all our own way. We can get swamped by our human ego; many do and will usually choose to repeat their lessons in a future life.

The physical death of the body is normally a pre-arranged event. The prior arrangement may be permissive: "You may live as long as you like," or contractual: "You may die young to give these people a reason to live without your support." Sharon Tate told me that her murder was by contract: "This was definitely planned." The big purpose of her brutal death was to draw public attention to the brainwashing and the way of life of current quasi-religious groups and cults.

Death may come as a freely made decision by the soul to withdraw from its current human life, the poet Sylvia Plath explained in our discussion. Death may be part of a large soul-group agreement, as Anne Frank experienced in Hitler's reign of terror. There, she told me, some of her soul mates who were, by prior agreement, on the Nazi side, assisted in her incarceration.

I questioned the Masters concerning the widely reported collapse of a bridge across the Mississippi River. Were any of the five deaths that resulted truly accidental? Their answer was that "there are no accidents." In every case, for one reason or another, the motorists who perished were on the bridge at that time to facilitate their death. In many cases, death comes because the soul has completed its assigned lessons and chooses to go Home. That may even happen in the case of children dying very young.

The Masters say "Transition" when speaking of our death. This word means "to change from one place or state of being to another." In human death two things happen: when the body itself ceases to live, it begins to disintegrate; the soul departs immediately from the body to another state of being. In this, however, there is more than one possibility.

In 2009, the Masters, Toni, and I began another book, bearing the title *How I Died (and what I did next)*. We had strong encouragement from the Masters, who provided contact with the souls we needed for the compilation of 25 stories. Regular people's souls from all over the world contributed to this study. I say this because these souls were people without fame or fortune. They may have left their physical body and live now in a different dimension, but hearing them talk, just as in the case of the leaders and celebrities whom we interviewed in our first three books, was exactly like talking with people we meet day by day.

The *How I Died* book's concept was to interview the souls of people who had lived and died in a wide variety of ways and circumstances, and who would represent many different nations and lifestyles. We asked them to tell how they came to die and what happened to their soul after the death of the body/shell.

From what the Masters told us, once the news got out about this publishing experiment, they were flooded out with crowds of souls wanting to tell their story. In a process of give and take with the Other Side, we worked out a basic list of situations. The first to give its story was a soul who recently had been incarnate as an African bushman who had a fatal accident while out hunting. He told us a graphic tale of how the poor man died a slow and painful death in the bush, then went with his grandfathers back Home to the Other Side. He was a family man, with a deep love of music, and the soul told us that it had previously lived a life in which he played the violin in an orchestra in Vienna.

Grandparents featured in more than one life. An innocent eight-year-old girl from a fisherman's family drowned in the awful 2004 Indonesian tsunami, then wandered about as a "discarnate" until her grandmother came to find her and take her Home. A discarnate is a soul who leaves the physical body but does not know how to get back to the spirits' realm, or fifth dimension, that we call "the Other Side" or chooses not to do so. Then it stays in the interface (my word) of the fourth dimension, between Earth and Home, until the problem is resolved. In the case of the fisherman's daughter who drowned in the tidal wave, it was mainly a matter of her soul not being fully aware that its human life had actually ended. Awareness of its physical death came slowly—but not as slowly as to some other souls I have interviewed, some of whom spent several Earth years living in the fourth dimension for various reasons.

Some of the stories that souls told were quite harrowing: the Vietnamese diplomat who was tortured and shot, the woman who faced death high up in the World Trade Center when it was destroyed on 9/11, and, deep underground, the British miner trapped by the collapse of a mine shaft and the rising waters in the area where he was working. Sometimes physical death was over quickly and, dare one say, simply, like the sudden end of the

Canadian philanthropist who did not see the bus that hit him, or the Brazilian playboy who "gave up" life after driving his Porsche over the edge of a cliff, and calmly watched while his car with his body in the driver's seat crashed on the rocks below.

Some deaths were easy, like the Greek woman innkeeper who died of a heart attack in her sleep, and the old French farmer who was quietly waiting for death in bed while her devout family was at Sunday mass. Her gentle departure was into the arms of her long-dead husband, her true love, who danced away with her over a celestial field of beautiful flowers.

Among those wo did not go Home so easily or happily was an American serial killer. Before his execution took place, the man had been persuaded by religious visitors to his cell on death row that he would burn in hell. When he died, he found himself in a state that conformed to their description—a place of fire and torment, where one might hear the shrieks and groans of the damned all around. He stayed in the fourth dimension for some years until, at last, he heard the quiet voice of his spirit guide suggesting that he turn down the heat and the noise, and—after that was successful—bringing him to the realization that hell was entirely created by his own mind and he could choose to go Home if he preferred. He did.

These are a few glimpses of a book that has brought me full circle in demystifying death and, therefore, diminishing the power of death in my consciousness. Most of the souls who told their story had suffered physically before death overwhelmed them. Dying can be a grisly business. Yet, even during their suffering, souls seemed to be readily able to disengage from their body, float free, and then take the hand of a loved one who had come to help them complete their journey and to lead them Home.

Now back Home, Elvis Presley's soul told me it is busy playing music to help little returning children feel welcomed. Anne

Frank's soul is doing valuable research in the Akashic records. Mother Teresa counsels others in need. Rachel Carson is giving spiritual support to environmental initiatives. No one seems to be bored or idle at Home. All are fulfilled as they live in their busy and unconditionally loving environment. That makes a world of sense. Some of the pageantry reserved for those who go to the Christian heaven: and stand around the throne of God with crowns on their heads, makes no sense. It was an idea passed down to us from a very different age. Here's the closing verse of *Love Divine, all loves excelling*. It is by Charles Wesley, the well-known eighteenth century hymn writer, and has a selection of at least five hymn tunes that are used regularly in Protestant churches.

> *"Finish, then, Thy new creation;*
> *Pure and spotless let us be.*
> *Let us see Thy great salvation*
> *Perfectly restored in Thee;*
> *Changed from glory into glory,*
> *Till in heaven we take our place,*
> *Till we cast our crowns before Thee,*
> *Lost in wonder, love, and praise."*

You should hear it sung in Welsh! But to which tune? It is not worth my while choosing for you. Vote for Blaenwern rather than Hyfrydol and ignore the rest? If you get it wrong, half your choir will walk out. And if you change your mind, the other half, plus the church organist will leave, I know: I've been there, done that! And when they return, don't mind if they bellow it in their joy.

Reincarnation

When interviewing souls for *How I Died*, what impressed me most was the enormous enthusiasm the Masters had for this literary project. They were really keen that humans might fully grasp the whole story of what happens to us at death and how we return to our spiritual base. Transition is truly the correct word to use when we are thinking about death—now we can actively *look forward* to the time when we will transition Home. This is not a message for good people, or people who have the right ideas, the correct faith. It is for every soul in every age.

It was all very new and exciting to be involved in teaching that insisted it was not religion and yet spoke with a clear voice about our purpose in living. I had instinctively discounted death as permanent and had believed from my youth in life after death, but had not known what rational explanation could be used to tell my peers about my belief: there was no way of proving anything. I came to embrace reincarnation as a rational answer for other people, as for myself. My wife Sonia, who had also taken hypnosis training, had read the same books, and was closely involved with my work with Toni, expressed a similar conviction. We live many lives as a spirit, in a succession of bodies and a wide variety of places both on planet Earth and elsewhere.

I'm still not at all accepting of a lot of speculative writing that is popular with some people. I'm quite sure that the vast majority of today's spiritual claims of enlightenment are being made in hope rather than in certainty. People have discovered that it is possible to win an audience and impress other people by being *spiritual,* embracing ideas even when they sound just a little bit unworldly. I guess it's the oldest trick in the book!

Following my Bliss

Now, having had the experience of working for years with the Ascended Masters as tutors, I will try to share my understanding of the Masters' message with you and enable you to understand your soul's journey. You will find that I have made no claims about myself in this book that might lead you to consider me a teacher of merit. Rather, I have taken pains to share with you how little I cared to conform to church norms in order to live my kind of life, and how I disregarded my youthful experiences and brushes with death that characterized my risk-prone self-centered way of living. I have not been "totally cool" as that girl claimed, but frequently stupid! That doesn't mean I have disliked life; on the contrary, it has generally been great fun.

Coming in from life's hurly burly to the relative quiet and calm of retirement, I find little things have happened all along the way that have prepared me for where I am now. You will be aware now that I got into hot water and made bad mistakes. Yet as the end of the walkabout comes into view, I'm sure the ingredients of my life have truly led me to the right place. The other day I asked the Masters if that was true. Their reply was typically opaque, but they did not disagree with this feeling. It is true; I have followed my bliss to the end of my spiritual walkabout.

When the young Aborigine sets off on walkabout, his excited thoughts are that his great adventure that will make him a man. He is now free from the villagers: the old men going on and on about the heritage of the tribe, his mother and aunts saying that he has a lot to learn about adult behavior before he becomes a man. Girls experience a change of status, when they marry and have babies at a very young age. Marriage is not a pressing matter for him. That's stuff the elders organized.

When the walkabout ends, I imagine a very different person arrives at the village square. Hardship has been real in the past months. It might have been the day he tripped, damaging his ankle, and will always limp in consequence. It might have been hunger or thirst, or snakes, or angry people in another village. He had depended on his ability to whistle to keep his spirits high. The songs of the villagers and his own individual song had sustained him. He had experienced the wisdom of dream time and his sacred animal's visiting him in his dreams. Now he knows that in the boot camp of the Outback he became a person in his own right. If that had not happened he would never have returned to the village; he would have died on the journey.

The spiritual walkabout of our twenty-first century society has some of the same ingredients. For me it involved departing from my parents' home, of my own free will and against my mother's wishes. I regarded that move as essential for personal freedom. Looking back, I know that I was less than kind in keeping in touch with my folks. I must have frustrated them greatly by my wanderlust, but now it still feels that it was the right thing to do. In a generation in Britain when the concept of the spiritual touched only lightly the lives of many of my peers, I went on wrestling with the questions of who I was, why I found myself where I was, and how I would be able to find the answers that would give me a clear direction in life. The problem was not so much that of following my bliss but of identifying what my bliss might be. The fact that I took seriously the spiritual element had a lot to do with my upbringing. Church and parents had given me a vision that I would be like the little acolyte in the temple hearing the divine voice call my name and tell me what to do. I heard nothing at the time, but eventually felt the presence of my loving, gentle soul.

There were streams to jump over, rock faces to climb on my way. It had not been easy to find a pathway. Agnosticism felt like a dead end, even though it had sharpened my skepticism and forced me to think things through. I would not have been as self-aware without the attitudes it displayed. Feeling free to do so, I attached myself to Jesus rather than to the church. Looking back on my years of ministry I found the church, as they said in the first century CE, *a stone to trip over* (New Testament Greek, *skandalon*, a stumbling block). The relative freedom of my denomination was an absolutely essential ingredient for my happiness. When the church council began to demand a greater obedience to the historic faith pronouncements of the Christian church, they lost me. I had never really thought of Jesus as divine. He was inspired, as others have been inspired, but not as unique as even I thought when first trying to follow his way of life.

My tribute to Jesus was finally paid when my small book, *Training for the Marathon of Life,* was published. This is a study, based on a much larger work by the scholars of the Jesus Seminar, of 50 core sayings they identified as most likely to have been said by Jesus. They had selected them from the four New Testament and from the very early Gospel of Thomas. Many other sayings in the gospels, considered by the biblical scholars were thought more likely to have been half-remembered or even lovingly invented to represent Jesus' thinking. I had found a clear plan for living in the Kingdom, and did my best to describe it. The slim book did not sell, because I'm a rotten salesperson.

Moving my ministry into the friendly General Assembly of Unitarian and Free Christian Churches brought relief, Here was a small liberal religious voice, with good ideas, but it was largely disregarded by society as an historical anomaly. In the heady days of the late nineteenth century when Charles Darwin's theories were hotly attacked and stoutly defended, the Unitarians were full of energy and their churches were packed. Then along came the Great War, followed by a huge rejection of religion by millions. Their leave-taking was felt more keenly among groups of religious liberals, who refused to force feed people with a theology in which spiritual discipline was stressed that Christians must believe unquestioningly in the triune god of Christianity. Those religious bodies, whose dogmas gave them a strong backbone and a powerful conviction that God called the church to combat sin and disbelief, did better than the liberals in the shakedown.

My later experience of the Unitarian Universalists in America was also reasonably enjoyable. There was no normative system of belief, simply a conviction that it was important for all of us to build our own theology, become aware of the nature of life, and deal with sensitive (or spiritual) issues as deserving of our attention. What the UUs did for me was to drain off much of the residual nonsense of Christian triumphalism. It prepared me for the Big Bang in my thinking and for the teaching of the Ascended Masters. And it was with the Masters that I came to the end of my journey, a very different person from when I was a young man setting off on my crazy spiritual walkabout. I had followed my bliss until it came to a halt: But it wasn't at the foot of the cross, where in *Pilgrim's Progress* John Bunyan saw the burden of sin falling from the back of Christian, the pilgrim. It had a lot to do with the incredible personal experience of communicating with the group of Ascended Masters in friendship. And it was friendship so far as I was concerned because we did not always see eye to eye. It was also a Homecoming in an loving sort of way.

The Masters' Teaching

At this point I want to give you a little of the Masters' teaching. It is printed in italics but is my personal version and not their words. They don't accept that what they tell us is "religion." They claim that their teaching is a presentation of the facts of the life that all souls experience, that we will all benefit from knowing. After all, we cannot ask the question "What is life?" without receiving some kind of cosmic explanation. Our mental pilgrimage begins with the Ascended Masters telling us about "Source."

Their teaching is too detailed to be reprinted here, so I will explain a little of it as best I can in my own words, anticipating that you may have not heard of the Masters before.

1. Source

Source energy is absolute perfection. This is described in terms humans can understand, as unconditional love. Source is pure nonphysical energy, not a person and not a divinity. The nonphysical energy of Source is the element that sustains all physical energy everywhere, without which nothing has ever existed. The nonphysical energy of Source is the only reality. Everything else that exists is an illusion created by Source.

Source is both absolutely perfect and also sentient. It may be described as the original mind.as Source wishes to understand itself at the deepest level possible. To fully understand its own magnificence, it chooses to examine its opposite—whatever Source energy is not. For this purpose it manifested the great universe in an energetic physical dimension other than its own eternal nonphysical self.

In physics the term "quantum" is used to express the smallest unit of any physical object. Let's look at a diamond in an engagement ring. A diamond is one of the most dense, tightly packed elements on Earth. That's why small, hard diamonds are used in cutting tools. Every diamond is composed of molecules that are groups of atoms. The word "atom" comes from an old Greek word meaning something that cannot be cut apart. In fact, internally, every atom is composed of a nucleus surrounded by a bunch of negatively charged electrons. The nucleus is itself composed of a quantum mix of even smaller sub-atomic particles, bound together by an electro-magnetic force. They circulate within each atom of the diamond. Most of the content of the atoms that together comprise the tough diamond is, in fact, empty space! This is a universal illusion as it appears to our senses, we only see matter: the reality is that the universe is simply energy.

I'm not a physicist, but the issue now is not that we understand completely how everything works, but grasp that physical matter, like the diamond, is not really what we see, feel, and wear, but an illusion created by forces and particles that we call energy. Not just diamonds but our nose, the Rocky Mountains, the moon, the Earth, and also ideas and emotions, thoughts and feelings, are really all energy.

The Masters teach that the sole *reality* is the energy of which everything is composed. The basic energy is Source energy. It is a fundamental part, for example, not only of physical matter, like diamonds, but of our thoughts. Source is, therefore, not a person, nor a god—it is absolutely pure nonphysical energy. In terms of its own nature it is absolutely positive. We identify that the most positive element, of which our human minds can conceive, is unconditional love. Present in everything that exists in the whole universe, this is the positive energy and being that we call Source.

Now I don't know about you, but I still get a little bewildered by this kind of talk. When people say "energy," I imagine a light bulb going on. When people talk about love, I picture a mother caring for her baby. Putting it all in absolute terms, as I've tried to do, makes it harder to picture. Fortunately, the rest of what we need to know is much easier to think about.

Let us press on: *"Being absolutely perfect, Source...wishes to know itself at the deepest level possible."* This is the mirror or the reflecting pool situation. If you had never seen yourself in a reflection, how would you truly feel about yourself? Without sight wouldn't you feel somewhat inadequate? Well, of course, blind people have that exact issue to overcome, and I guess that they will confirm how wonderful it would be if they could see their appearance. How do blind people find out what they look like? Two possibilities are learning by touch and by asking others who can see them. But all that is only how people *appear* to others. How can we measure *who we really are* without having someone to explain the idea?

Source energy has the quality of thoughtfulness—sentience. This has led Source to examine what it really is by creating situations unlike itself. This is rather like bringing the blind to be with other people who can see them and tell them what they look like. This discovery is the intention that Source has—but who can tell Source what unconditional love is and is not? The answer to that conundrum is to be found next.

2. Souls

Source also creates individual parts of itself, which are like droplets of sea spray in an ocean of energy. These fragments of

Source, which we call souls, are detached from Source in respect of the work they do and the unique personality they develop, but continue to share in the nature and energy of Source, to which they always remain connected, and which enables them energetically to exist as nonphysical energies.

Souls are given total freedom by Source to gain the knowledge they seek in whatever way seems best to them. Their intention is to develop their knowledge—a fresh view of what Source is <u>not</u> like—which may be brought back Home so that the wisdom of Source is enriched.

When Source detaches souls, groups of individual souls form, and these energetic entities work together as soul mates in collecting wisdom from the variety of experiences they all have. As they do their work, individual souls choose partners for mutual support. Over the course of many lives on Earth, souls play a variety of roles, helped by their working partners.

I grew up with the idea of God as a person outside of myself. Maybe you may have held that view as well. So we ask God for help, share our troubles with God, and sing our praises to this divine being. We need to think of Source quite differently. Not as a person outside of us, Source is energy in which our souls themselves are living in Oneness, a state of true unity.

Our individuality is purely functional. The foaming spray on a wave appears to comprise separate droplets until the wave has fallen and is contained in the sea again. In the same way, our souls leave Home's dimension of unconditional love and venture out on journeys with the purpose of bringing back knowledge they have gained on their own. But, in fact, they are never fully on their own. Not only do souls work together in teams, but a portion of each soul's energy is always left behind at Home, giving it constant access to the Source energy of which it is a small particle.

3. Planet Earth

Souls spend time in various parts of the universe to develop their skills and enrich their knowledge. In some situations they remain cloud-like bundles of energy; in Earth and some other places they visit, it is necessary for them to have a physical body, or "shell." It depends on the environment they are in.

Source wished to have experience of whatever is found to be its opposite so that a comparison can be made. In order to evaluate its own nature most clearly, it made planet Earth available for souls to visit and for this purpose the planet was deliberately created to have a "duality" a fine-tuned equal balance of positive and negative energies. This provides the opportunities for the most searching tests individual souls ever undertake.

Planet Earth is itself a spiritual entity. As is well known to human science, all its physical elements are composed of energetic particles. The planet has life cycles that cleanse and renew it, and has sentient feelings concerning the life that is lived on its surface. It supports a polar environment, with energy controlling all the positive and negative elements experienced by souls.

Think of an old-fashioned pair of scales, with two bowls hanging by little chains from a bar, with a pointer that shows which side is most weighed down. When the weight of one side matches the other, the pointer will register a perfect balance. Planet Earth is finely balanced between positive energy, of which souls are one of the elements, and on the other side, negative energy. There is nothing "good" and "bad" in that balance. We don't call black holes in space bad, even when they are busy swallowing stars. They are just negative. Think of a magnet: one end is a positive pole that attracts metal objects, and the other end is negative that repels metal objects. Neither is better or worse than the other. This lack of judgment permeates the entire universe so heaven and hell are purely states of mind humans possess from time to time in their lives, not a result of judgment.

In their quest to gain knowledge for Source, souls visit many places in the universe. On planet Earth they must do so by taking a human body/shell (the Masters' own term). This equipment is needed for the same reason—their survival—which is why an astronaut dons a space suit to walk on the moon. The human body with its ego and conscious mind is the soul's space suit that it needs while it is incarnate on Earth. The knowledge souls seek is about the negative elements of existence, not only those that appear "bad" to the human mind, but also those that are judgmental, a state of being that is unknown in the spiritual dimension.

4. Incarnation

Souls freely choose to incarnate on Earth rather like actors undertaking various roles in a drama. They freely choose in advance the overall lessons they wish to learn that will increase their wisdom; freely make contracts with soulmates to provide or receive experiences that may be valuable; and they freely choose the environment into which they will come and, importantly, who will be their parents. In some cases souls deliberately opt to live a human life, in whole or in part, that is dedicated to creating negativity. At other times they will accept a situation in which the human being they inhabit will suffer from dire negative experiences not of its creation. Most souls choose a role in life that has both positive and negative elements.

Souls usually choose to vary the types of experiences they undertake over the course of several incarnations. They will be male or female, straight or gay, belong to many different races, live in different parts of the planet, be born into families that provide the whole range of talent, education, wealth, religious conviction, and social status. The freedom of choice that each soul exercises in these matters is respected completely. While there are peer counselors who assist with a soul's plans made in advance of incarnation, the soul is always in charge of its own destiny and remains free to change its mind once it has actually become a human being.

The process of incarnation follows a regular path. The soul is aware of the conception of the body/shell it will inhabit and retains an energetic marker to the fetus. Most souls enter the body of the fetus shortly before birth takes place. This timing is easier for the soul and avoids situations in which, because of the physical death of the fetus, the soul would have to release itself from the body. Before the soul takes over from the mother, the fetus is kept alive by her energy. No human being can otherwise sustain life without the indwelling energy of a soul.

The most difficult issue for us to understand about incarnation (taking a physical body) is the issue of our choosing negative roles. What lovely soul, we ask, would ever want to choose to be a flesh and blood serial killer, a Stalin or Hitler, a pedophile, or an abusive husband? Yet we go to see movies where actors do just that, and we sometimes comment on the fine skill of the actor in portraying the villain so well!

Souls take negative-life roles in order to learn what it is to be "inside" a negative person. They choose to suffer abuse in order to understand the nature of negativity. Human beings see things in terms of black and white, good and bad, right and wrong. Human beings are locked into making judgments, and some religions say that the world ends with a Day of Judgment. In fact judgment is not something souls experience or use. They may well evaluate the effectiveness of something, but there is no good and evil in their vocabulary, and there is no wrathful, avenging deity sending people to hell. Hell is a state of mind here on Earth and, as such, is sometimes predictably an experience, chosen in advance by a soul for its human self to have: but hell is never a punishment from a God for evil done.

What we have to focus our mind on is that souls are acting out parts to be played that have been chosen by them, freely and in advance, in what I call for fun the actors' greenroom at Home. No one made me kill Robin or Muffy. No one made me screw up two marriages. No one forced me to engage in risky behavior. My soul chose those roles so it might grow wise examining them in the light of unconditional love.

We come to planet Earth and pour our life-sustaining energy into a little fetus, with a laundry list of lessons to learn and a clutch of fellow souls to provide help. In each lifetime we make contracts with soulmates so that either we or they will provide the negative experiences that we all need, and the mentally challenging lessons that will help us to grow in knowledge and wisdom. That is the purpose of it all, and why we are here in the bruising environment of planet Earth. The Buddha was right to categorize life in terms of suffering, but it is not the soul who suffers, for the soul is an actor with a puppet and the world its stage. It is only the human part of the incarnation which suffers.

The end of the walkabout

There is a great deal more in the teaching of the Ascended Masters. Toni, Sonia, and I now have published books that taken together attempt to paint the whole picture. The journey of the soul has been known to seers, mystics, philosophers, and people of faith. They were our forerunners in gaining some of the knowledge expressed in this book. Now, helped from the various studies mentioned here, we have a good map of where our spiritual walkabout will take us.

Returning to my "village," with my walkabout nearly complete for this lifetime, I may still have more to experience but no longer have my whole life ahead of me. I guess many people will have done the journey faster, and more successfully. This journey could have reached a dead end early on had I embraced agnosticism, or had become an evangelical Protestant or a Roman Catholic. I could have been more fearful of death, and might have been more structured in my path through life. There are plenty of other might-have-been scenarios each of us can imagine, but you have been told mine and now it's your turn to puzzle out what kind of spiritual walkabout you have taken.

In the end we follow our bliss, take on the role that suits us and try to create the life that fulfills us. Now, as I break the tape at the age of eighty,(having come to a full stop physically), the rest of my life this time around will probably be short. I will transition from the current play on the world's stage, back to the celestial green room in the fifth dimension that spirits call Home. And I am sure my soul will not mind coming back and taking another spiritual walkabout. There is a lot to learn down here on planet Earth.

Peter Watson Jenkins

Books by authors mentioned in this memoir

Pacifism: A selection of books is available on Amazon. Search for: Books: Fellowship of Reconciliation.

The trial and Death of Socrates by Plato. Many translations available. The reference in this book was to the *Crito* section.

The Dream of Gerontius: Many CD recordings are available of the oratorio by Sir Edward Elgar. Cardinal Newman's text is included.

Battle for the Mind by William Sargent is in several editions.

A Chosen Faith: An Introduction to Unitarian Universalism by John Buehrens, Forrest Church, Denise Davidoff and Robert Fulghum.

Life after Life: The Investigation of a Phenomenon--Survival of Bodily Death by Raymond Moody and Elisabeth Kubler-Ross

Many Lives, Many Masters: The True Story of a Prominent Psychiatrist, His Young Patient, and the Past-Life Therapy... by Brian L. Weiss

Journey of Souls: Case Studies of Life between Lives by Michael Newton

Where Reincarnation and Biology Intersect by Ian Stevenson
Twenty Cases Suggestive of Reincarnation by Ian Stevenson

Life before Life by Helen Wambach
Reliving Past Lives: The Evidence under Hypnosis by Helen Wambach

Metaphysical books by Peter Watson Jenkins channeled by Toni Ann Winninger.

Exploring Reincarnation

How I died (and what I did next)

Life Lessons, Our purpose in being human

Listening to Spirit Wisdom

Spirit World Wisdom

Talking with Leaders of the Past

Talking with Twentieth-Century Men

Talking with Twentieth-Century Women

In preparation

The Message of the Ascended Masters

Books by Peter Watson Jenkins

A thriller: *Escape to Danger*

Past-life regression: *Christy's Journey*

Short-story collection: *Found Money*

Theology: *Training for the Marathon of Life*

Young Adult romance/adventure: *Saved by a Tweet*

In preparation

Poetry and prose: *Fine Writing* (in 2015)

Sci-fi: *How the Masters Rescued Planet Earth* (in 2015)

These books are available from Amazon and from bookshops that access the Ingram catalogue. Most are available as ebooks. We also sell them at: www.celestialvoicesinc.com

CPSIA information can be obtained
at www.ICGtesting.com
Printed in the USA
FFOW03n1720131015
17638FF

9 780983 601692